Now You Tell Me!
What I Wish I'd Known Before I Got Married

2020
By Jeff Berger

Other books by Jeff Berger:
Finding Jesus (2019)
Hark the Herald Angels Sing, A Christmas Devotional (2015)

Dedicated to Carrie. It has been an adventure, and I'm glad we're on it together!

Table of Contents

Introduction: Why Should You Read This? 5

Chapter 1: Your Soul Mate Doesn't Exist 8

Chapter 2: Never Dig a Foxhole 13

Chapter 3: Become an Expert on Your Spouse 18

Chapter 4: Marriage Wasn't Designed to Make You Happy 27

Chapter 5: Sex is Not Simple 33

Chapter 6: Competition is a Curse 42

Chapter 7: There is a Right Way to Fight 53

Chapter 8: Pray Constantly For Her 60

Chapter 9: You Can't Do This Alone 66

Chapter 9 ½: Randomness 76

Chapter 10: Love Don't Come Easy 80

Introduction

Why Should You Read This?

Alright, so...cards on the table: I am not an expert on the subject of marriage. I am not a trained marriage counselor, a psychologist or a licensed therapist. Nor do I have the perfect marriage. My wife Carrie and I have been married since the week after our college graduation, and we've had our share of difficulties in the years since. I can honestly (and gratefully) say that our relationship is a huge source of joy in my life, the second-best thing that has ever happened to me. But as I look back over the journey from our wedding day to today, I see so many mistakes I made. Truth be told, I'll make more mistakes before the whole "death do us part" thing kicks in. So why am I writing this? I'm not just a guy who's been married over half his life; I'm also a pastor. I know from decades in the ministry that other couples struggle as much as we have...and more.

It comes down to this: There are so many hard-won lessons I wish I could share with my younger self, so that I could avoid the pain of those mistakes. That's the way this book is laid out: Each chapter is based on something I would say to my younger, unmarried self if I could. But, since I possess neither a DeLorean nor a Flux Capacitor, time travel is impossible (and even if I did, there's that whole "messing up the space-time continuum" thing). The next best thing I can do is share these lessons with others.

If you're married and struggling, please understand that this is not a book about how to change your spouse. I would strongly advise you to give up on that project, anyway. I do hope my words bring you hope. Your troubles don't define you as a bad person. Nor do they mean your marriage is doomed. You can't make your spouse change, but you can bring something new to your relationship. Try it and see what happens!

If you are happily married, congratulations! Don't become complacent. I hope that what I've written here can help you avoid some of the pitfalls that torpedo relationships...and make a good thing even better.

If you are single and hope to be married someday, know this: the character, habits and priorities you're forming now will determine what kind of marriage you'll have. Now is the time to grow into the person your future spouse will need.

This book is written from a Christian perspective. Will it help people of other faiths, or no faith at all? I think so. But I am infinitely more confident in this: The God of the Bible, the One who came to earth in the form of the man Jesus Christ, invented marriage. He created marriage long before any nation or organized religious system existed. Marriage is important to Him…not just the concept of marriage, but your marriage, and mine. So it stands to reason that following this God is the best way to build a healthy, fulfilling marital relationship. That doesn't mean that simply believing Christian doctrine and going to church will guarantee you wedded bliss. Nor does it mean that non-Christians cannot build loving, lasting marriages. So what do I mean? Well…

Despite what most people (including many Christians) believe, the Christian faith is not simply a religion; it's more than rules, rituals, and doctrinal principles. It's a journey. Read the Gospels (The books of Matthew, Mark, Luke and John) sometime, and you'll notice that Jesus never asked people to join a religion, to commit to a creed, or to follow a list of laws. Instead, when Jesus met people, He simply said, "Follow me." That is still the case today. When we follow Jesus, we are born again. Our journey through life takes a sudden, new trajectory. We're now on a road that ends in Heaven, in the presence of His perfect love forever. As we continue to follow Him on this road, we become more like Him each step of the way. And because He loves marriage, these changes in us make us better husbands and wives. It's a beautiful thing to see, and a magnificent thing to experience. If you'd like to know more about what it means to follow Jesus, I've written another book, *Finding Jesus*, about that exact subject. Or, even better, read the New Testament. If you would like to follow Him, tell Him so. He's ready to start that journey with you…and He'll take you, right now, just as you are. Christians aren't people who've worked out all their sins and achieved perfection; they're people who have realized they'll never be perfect, and need grace. If you'd like to talk this over, check in with a local church. You can contact my church by visiting www.fbcconroe.org.

Let's get started!

Chapter 1

Your Soul Mate Doesn't Exist

Here's a statement that's impossible to prove: No one has ever been more in love than I was at twenty-one years old. I know, I know. But you should have seen me. If present-day me (or anyone else) had said to twenty-one-year-old me, "There is no such thing as a soul mate," I would have disagreed passionately. In my young adulthood, I thought with all my heart that there was one special woman God had chosen for me…just like there was one special person for everyone. Furthermore, I was absolutely certain I had found her. And since God had brought us together, we would have a marriage so blissful, so perfect, the world would stand amazed.

Where did I get such an idea? I was a committed Christian at that time, but my opinions on this subject didn't come from Scripture. Instead, the "soul mate" concept is rooted in ancient Greek thought. As Plato put it: "…and when one of them meets the other half, the actual half of himself, whether he be a lover of youth or a lover of another sort, the pair are lost in an amazement of love and friendship and intimacy and one will not be out of the other's sight, as I may say, even for a moment…" I found that quote on a website called "The 45 Best Soulmate Quotes." Yes, apparently that's a thing. Our culture loves the idea that there is a perfect person for each of us out there somewhere. It's the main idea behind most romantic movies; note that movies almost never focus on what it takes to make a relationship last. Can you name the last movie you saw about a married couple trying to stay together? Instead, they tend to be about the obstacles a man and woman have to overcome in order to find each other and fall in love. It's all about the dashing Prince placing the glass slipper on Cinderella's foot, not on what life is like for Cindy and her man five years later, when there are bills to pay, kids to feed, and the Fairy Godmother is nowhere to be found.

Our song lyrics feed this notion as well. The most common theme in popular music is "true love," which means finding that person you were destined for, who makes life worth living. Talk to unmarried people, and you'll see we have completely bought into this idea. In our minds, the soul mate we're looking for is someone who will meet all of our expectations in a lover, without asking us to change in any way. We're looking for the ideal version of ourselves, only in the body of an attractive member of the opposite sex…who also happens to be crazy about us.

For twenty-one-year-old me, it was even worse, because I had made this idea part of my theology. In my defense, there was an entire cottage industry devoted to nurturing this concept: I call it the Christian-Marital Industrial Complex. My engagement and early marriage days were during a time when Bible-believing Christians were so eager to build up the institution of marriage, our leaders over-sold some ideas. One was the idea that Christians, especially committed believers, and ESPECIALLY Christians who had put off sexual intimacy until their wedding day, had happier marriages (including more torridly satisfying sex lives) than unbelievers. Joel Gregory in his book *Too Great a Temptation* tells the story of his predecessor at First Baptist, Dallas, the legendary WA Criswell, preaching a sermon on this very subject. Criswell referenced some recent studies about marital satisfaction among Christians, baptized it in Scripture, and his takeaway line was, "Young men, marry a First Baptist woman. She'll love you so good, they'll have to carry you off in a wheelbarrow." The huge congregation was initially stunned at hearing such saucy stuff from their white-haired patriarch, but after a moment's silence, the place went up in laughter. That message was forevermore known as "the wheelbarrow sermon." Interestingly, Gregory reports that when people asked Mrs. Criswell what she thought if it, she said, "WA doesn't know what he's talking about."

But I thought I knew. I had found a stunningly beautiful, Christ-centered woman who had agreed to marry me. We had done everything right, as far as I could tell. We were destined for marital greatness.

And then we got married.

I won't go into detail about the first year of our marriage. I will simply say this: I was devastated at how hard it was. So much so, I questioned God. How could He do this to me? I had tried to do things His way. Didn't He owe me happiness as a result? We had rarely argued during our two-and-a-half years of dating and engagement; now we fought constantly. For years, she had been the person I couldn't do without. I had driven an hour each way to see her three times each weekend. Now, we often couldn't stand the sight of each other. It's almost as if getting married was the worst possible thing that could happen to our relationship.

I learned two invaluable lessons that year: One, **I couldn't look to her as the source of my happiness**. Marriage doesn't work like that. No human being can bear that weight. The infatuation of the early days of falling in love is thrilling. So is the anticipation of an engagement. But those kinds of feelings are temporary. It's like eating the most spectacular dessert ever; it tastes amazing, but you can't live on it long-term. But there is something more substantial out there. He called Himself the Bread of Life (John 6:35) and promised that in Him—and only in Him—is true, lasting satisfaction and fulfillment. I believed in Him before, but now I turned to Him in desperation. The second thing I learned that year was, **in order for this marriage to work, I had to change…and so did she**. We both needed to grow out of our selfishness and pettiness, and the sooner, the better.

It wasn't enough that I had fallen in love. Any idiot can do that. It wasn't even enough that we were both Christians. That year, I embarked on a long process of learning what it meant to become a good man. I'm still working on that. The good news is that, over the years, we have built something wonderful. I look forward to seeing her each day, and the high point of my week is our Friday breakfast date. I look back over these years together, and see so many ways she has supported me, sacrificed for me, helped me choose the right path, and filled my days with joy and laughter. It took work for us to get to this point, but it has been well worth it.

I remember seeing a published study in the years just after I stopped believing in soulmates. It said that people who were in arranged marriages had far greater marital satisfaction than people who chose their own mates. It's hard for us in the Global West to believe such a claim. We think personal freedom is essential to happiness, including the freedom to choose one's own spouse. But as I thought about it, it made sense. A man in an arranged marriage knows that he is stuck with this woman, so he might as well learn to love her for who she is. He has no reason to compare her to some mythical person who meets all his needs; he went into the relationship without those overly romantic expectations. So whereas the American model leaves him thinking, "My soulmate is out there somewhere. I just married the wrong person," his actual situation leaves him with one viable option: Love the one he has. And build something beautiful with her.

I'm not arguing that we should begin arranging marriages for our kids (although as a Dad, the idea is appealing). But here's what I am saying:

If you're not married, don't assume that your future happiness is guaranteed by marrying the right person—or being married at all. A life of singleness is not an empty life (see 1 Corinthians 7, where Paul calls his singleness a gift), and is far better than marrying someone for the wrong reasons. Before you marry, ask yourself, "Does he/she make me a better person?" From a Christian perspective, that means "Does he/she draw me closer to Christ, and to becoming the person He is trying to create in me?" Ask someone who knows you well that same question–your parents or a close friend who will definitely tell you the truth. If the answer is no, walk away. If the answer is yes, and you choose to marry…it will still be hard work! I would have absolutely answered "yes" to that question, and it has still been incredibly difficult! But the work will be so very worth it.

If you are married, there is a person God has in mind for you to love, to believe in, to support, to pray for, to seek to please, and to enjoy completely. That person is the person to whom you are currently married. There is no exception to that statement. Ask God to help you love them as they are, to love them as He does. In other words, ask God to help you love your spouse the way He already loves you. He sees all the flaws, but He chooses to love you anyway. In fact, against all the odds, He delights in you. And He can produce that kind of love in your marriage, too. Give Him that chance…and then go to work building something beautiful.

Action Steps:
1. If you're single, you probably have a mental list of attributes you're looking for in a marriage partner. Write the list out. For every item on your list, ask yourself these questions: "Is this characteristic in my spouse necessary for my spiritual and emotional health, or is it simply something I would prefer?" Then separate your characteristics into "Preferences" and

"Non-negotiables." Show your list to a trusted friend (preferably one who is married) to see what he/she thinks. Revise as needed.

2. If you are in a dating relationship, ask trusted friends, "Do you like me more since I've been with this person, or less? Why?" Promise them you won't be angry with them no matter what they say…and keep that promise.

3. If you are married, your "list of qualifications" for a spouse needs to vanish forever. Your spouse will find him/herself competing against a mythical person, and will always lose that competition. Anytime you find yourself thinking, "I would be happy if only my spouse were more _____," that is idolatry. Confess it before God, and help Him to teach you to love your spouse as he/she is. Keep on praying that same prayer until your mental "list" is gone, and you begin to appreciate the person you married.

Chapter 2

Never Dig a Foxhole

In our first chapter, we demolished the myth of the soul mate. No matter how perfectly compatible you and your spouse may be, marriage will still be hard work. But why? Why is it so difficult for two people to live together in a love relationship for a lifetime? In my experience as a husband and a pastor, I have seen one factor more than any other divide husbands and wives. You might think it's money, workaholism, intrusive in-laws, one spouse's wandering eye, bad temper, or ESPN. Actually, in my opinion, Lifetime Network and HGTV are far worse for a marriage than televised sports. Just kidding! Sort of. None of those forces equals the sheer destructive power of this one thing:

Would you believe that your marriage's worst enemy is you?

Specifically, your tendency justify yourself, to see yourself as the only reasonable person in the relationship, while casting your spouse in the role of the stubborn fool, the mentally delusional nutjob, or the garden-variety jerk.

Here's a confession: I stink at marriage counseling. It took me a while to realize this, because I love being a pastor. I love most parts of my job so much, I'd do them even if I wasn't paid. So when married couples have approached me, asking if I could help them work through some problems they were having, I've always been glad to do what I could. But afterwards, I rarely felt I had actually helped them. Often, I knew these people well. They were friends. I liked and respected them. Surely, I

thought, this will be simple, just letting them talk things through, offering a few pieces of sage advice, and praying for healing. They would thank me and walk away with their love for each other renewed. It never seemed to work out that way. Instead, I would find one partner tearfully, bitterly rehearsing the offenses she has had to put up with, the Hell on Earth she has been experiencing. Meanwhile, the other spouse looks absolutely astonished. He can't understand why she gets to play the victim, when she is far from perfect herself (It wasn't always the wife accusing and the husband on defense, but for ease of reading, I will leave the gender pronouns this way). He offers semi-sincere apologies, promises to try harder, and basically minimizes her complaints. They leave angrier than they were when they arrived.

After years of this, I finally realized something: By the time couples came to me for marriage counseling, they were already past the point of wanting to "work on their marriage." They had each dug a foxhole, and their relationship had degenerated into lobbing occasional grenades at each other. Her motive in coming to me for counseling was simply an attempt to get a third party to confirm what she had been saying to him all along. She wanted me to say, "No woman should have to put up with what you've gone through." Whereas he was hoping I would join in with his self-defense, telling her, "Get over it; he's not so bad." Each wanted me to climb into their foxholes and fight alongside them. Any advice I offered would be politely received. But I got the distinct feeling that they both were thinking, "Preacher, you obviously haven't been listening to me. I'm not the one who needs to change, my spouse is."

I want to make something clear: I am not diminishing the pain these people felt. The problems they expressed were real (Another point of clarity: We weren't talking about abuse), and the pain they felt was profound. Tears were shed. These conversations were agonizing, for them and for me. But in every case, I walked away thinking, "Surely two people bound together by a common commitment to Christ, who've raised children together and had years of experience with each other, can work through this." And often, the answer was no, they couldn't. Or perhaps wouldn't. They had crossed a threshold, some point of no return. Their separate foxholes were too well-fortified. Only unconditional surrender on the part of their spouse (adversary?) could possibly stave off the inevitable divorce.

Side note: Another thing I learned from this experience–and which I am anxious to share with you–is that a trained counselor is worth every dollar it would cost you to see him. Your pastor, a family member or trusted friend can listen, offer advice and prayers, and there is value in that...but it's not a replacement for someone who does this for a living. Find a professional to talk to, and do it BEFORE you've got one foot out the door.

A few years ago, I read something that distilled these scattered, frustrated thoughts for me. Someone expressed what I've been feeling perfectly. In their book *Mistakes Were Made (But Not By Me)*, social psychologists Carol Tavris and Elliot Aronson wrote:

"The vast majority of couples who drift apart do so slowly, over time, in a snowballing pattern of blame and self-justification. Each partner focuses on what the other one is doing wrong, while justifying his or her own preferences, attitudes, and ways of doing things. ... From our standpoint, therefore, misunderstandings, conflicts, personality differences, and even angry quarrels are not the assassins of love; self-justification is."

In other words, it's a foxhole mentality: "I'm the good guy here. I have to take these steps to protect myself from her. When I engage her, it's an effort to gain some ground in our struggle, to balance things out a little bit."

I'm ashamed to admit it, but I've seen this in my own attitude toward my wife. When I am upset with her, my frustration feels like the most legitimate, reasonable emotion I could possibly feel. There's a voice essentially saying, "You SHOULD be mad! Anyone else would be! In fact, anyone else would have been fed up long ago!" On the other hand, I see my own faults as a husband as no big deal. I've got a boatload of excuses: "Her expectations are unreasonable." "She knew I was that way when she married me." "All things considered, I'm still a lot better than most guys she could be married to." I guess you could say I've spent time in both foxholes. I've played my share of offense and defense. My marriage's worst enemy is me.

So what is the answer? Simply put, the only sure answer is the Gospel. I don't mean that converting to Christianity will fix your marriage. Christians have this problem just as much as non-Christians do, because we still have a sin nature. I mean we have to let the Gospel take over our marriages. Here's what I mean:

In Luke 18:9-14, Jesus told a story about a morally upright, devoutly religious man who went to the temple to pray, and happened to see a notorious sinner there, a man who made his living scamming his own people. The pious brother prayed a pious prayer: *God, I thank you that I am not like other people–robbers, adulterers, evildoers–or even like this tax collector. I fast twice a week and give a tenth of all I get.* That man was doing what we do in marriage–self-justifying. He was saying, "I'm not the problem, HE is." He was saying, "I'm so much better than most men, my flaws aren't even worth mentioning." He was playing offense and defense. But Jesus told us the prayer of the other man, too: *God, have mercy on me, a sinner.* The Lord then said something that must have astonished his hearers: *I tell you that this man, rather than the other, went home justified. For those who exalt themselves will be humbled, and those who humble themselves will be exalted.* It's a little-known fact about our faith: Christianity doesn't make us perfect (at least, not yet). It makes us repentant. Christians aren't better people than non-Christians; but they should be much more aware of their own failings than others. That's how we are saved in the first place; not by promising to try really hard to be good, but by admitting we've failed and asking Him to take over. That's how we grow into the people we were made to be.

So how does this work in marriage? Whenever we feel ourselves moving towards "It's HIS fault!" or "Why does she ALWAYS overreact?" we must recognize that as self-justification. That's the voice of the Pharisee, drawing us further away from God…and further away from our spouse. I discovered years ago that the more I focus on things I'd like to change in my wife, the unhappier I am. After all, a self-centered eye can find fault in anyone, and can magnify those thoughts to the point of making us miserable. But when I begin to focus instead on overcoming my own flaws, working against my selfish, lazy tendencies, and trying to be the man she deserves, I am happier. Counterintuitively, I begin to see in her all the reasons I married her in the first place…and discover some new ones I never noticed before. Here's another way to put it: **If your main goal is to turn your spouse into the person you want him/her to be, it will always end badly. If your main goal in marriage is to learn to love your spouse as he/she is right now, you will succeed.** Why? Because that's God's goal for you, too, and He's working alongside you.

If you are struggling in marriage right now, my words may seem ridiculous. But I ask you to consider this: **What would it look like if you**

climbed out of your foxhole and met your spouse on neutral ground? Imagine what might happen if you sat him/her down and said (without mentioning any of your grievances), "Here are the ways I know I have let you down. And here's how I want to improve." Or even, "If I could do anything to make our marriage better for you, what would it be?" Does that sound impossible? It probably does. Getting out of a foxhole in the middle of a war zone always does. But it's the only way to make peace. Someone has to take that risk. Everything within you will resist; we enjoy feeling like the victim. But when we first fell in love, we had dreams of a wonderful life together. I believe those dreams are still worth fighting for; only the enemy is not the person in the other foxhole, it's us.

Action Steps

1. If you're married, consider the foxhole analogy. Does that apply to your relationship with your spouse? How often do you see yourself as the "good" guy and him/her as the one completely at fault? Be honest with yourself.

2. Pray and ask God to help you see your marriage—and any conflict that exists between you--through your spouse's eyes.

3. What would it look like for you to climb out of your foxhole? In other words, how could you show your spouse, "I take seriously the ways I have hurt you and let you down?" What are the risks? What good could come from it? What's stopping you?

Chapter 3

Become an Expert on Your Spouse

The comedian Jim Gaffigan has a bit about the saying, "It ain't brain surgery." When most people want to say something is easy, they compare it to brain surgery, because that's something very difficult. Gaffigan wonders what brain surgeons say instead. Perhaps, "It ain't like trying to talk to women."

Then there's the old joke about the guy who manages to conjure a genie, who offers him a wish. The man says, "I'd like a bridge from California to Hawaii, so that I could drive there anytime I want." The genie replies, "Come on. Do you know how impractical that is? Think of the wasted resources, not to mention what it would do to the environment. Choose something else." So the man thinks a moment. "Well, I've always wanted to understand women…" The genie quickly says, "So you want two lanes or four on that bridge?"

Recently, a friend sent me a clever saying in an email, "Women spend more time wondering what men are thinking than men do thinking."

It's conventional wisdom that men and women cannot possibly understand one another. People often validate this idea by saying, "After all, as the book says, Men Are from Mars, and Women Are from Venus." I highly doubt these people have ever read said volume (full disclosure: neither have I), but they take that title as a documented fact. I say baloney. I'm not saying that I understand women—as if all women have the same thoughts, desires or goals. I am saying that it's possible for A man to understand A woman, and vice-versa. Actually, without that understanding, it's nearly impossible to have a happy, healthy marriage.

Perhaps you're skeptical. You've looked with bafflement at the opposite gender for years, or perhaps you're married and think that your spouse is the most inscrutable oddball on the planet. Maybe I am just a hopeless romantic. But I tend to believe there is something to the fact that in Hebrew (the language of the Old Testament), the word used for sexual intercourse (the act that consummates a marriage) is a word that means "to know." (As it happens, the Hebrew word is *yada*. Seinfeld fans might find that humorous) God didn't create marriage as a relationship in which two people share a home, produce some offspring, and tolerate each other. It's His desire that I truly know my wife and am known by her, in a way that isn't true of any other person on earth.

How do we get there? Gary Chapman's *The Five Love Languages: The Secret to Love That Lasts* is a book that I wish I had read before I got married. According to Chapman, the "in love" stage of a romantic relationship lasts an average of two years. During that "in love" period, the object of your affection can seemingly do no wrong. Every gift, every note, every affectionate gesture is like a treasure. And you are thrilled to do those things for them, as well. But after that stage passes, we begin to want more from them. Chapman says that's because every person has a primary "language" that they use to express AND receive love. You might think you're doing the same sorts of things you did when the two of you first fell in love, but your spouse doesn't appreciate them anymore. Meanwhile, your spouse seems to have stopped making you feel the way you did in the "good old days." As they used to say, "The thrill is gone." A young man once spoke to me about his marriage. He could not understand why his wife was so unhappy with him. "I bring her flowers constantly. We've got pots lined up in our kitchen cabinets from all the bouquets I've brought home to our apartment." Gently, I said, "Maybe she doesn't want flowers." His wife was a highly practical person. I knew she was frustrated with him because she thought he wasn't trying hard enough to find a job. The flowers were, to her, a meaningless gift intended to distract her from the real issue. What he meant as an act of love was received by her as an insult. If you understand your spouse's love language, you then know how to make them feel loved. And, Chapman asserts, a spouse who truly feels loved will love you in return.

Chapman's book should be required reading for all married couples. He actually has some great free resources on his website (5lovelanguages.com) as well, including a test you and your spouse can take to find out your love languages. Let's look at the love languages he has identified:

Words of affirmation. 1 Thessalonians 5:11 commands us, *Therefore encourage one another and build one another up.* The Greek word for "encourage" means "to come alongside." Picture a long-distance runner who is at the point of quitting, when suddenly, a friend comes running alongside, encouraging her to finish the race. The Greek word for "to build up" is a construction term for building a structure. In other words, thoughtful words can do more than make us feel better; they can help us fulfill our potential, the same way a contractor takes blueprints and makes them a brick-and-mortar building. This is especially true for people with this love language. Whereas public praise might embarrass others, it makes these people visibly brighten. They keep greeting cards and notes of encouragement forever. They choose their own words carefully, wordsmithing emails and notes to friends and family. On the other hand, a harsh word can damage them more deeply than the rest of us. Insults, criticisms and accusations stick with them for a long time. Giving them "the silent treatment" is unbearable. Refusing to return an "I love you" is like a knife in the heart.

If your spouse has this love language, find a reason to praise them for something every day. You'll learn what they find most meaningful…and where they are most vulnerable. In general men don't want to be teased about their courage or physical strength, and women find jokes about their weight or appearance to be off-limits, but your spouse has other areas where he or she feels insecure. Know them. Bragging about your spouse in front of others is especially powerful. When I was twelve, I hurt my wrist on the playground. I played in two Little League baseball games before I found out I had a hairline fracture. Later, I heard my dad telling a group of men how tough I was. Decades later, I still remember how good that made me feel. Writing your kind words down is a good move, as well. Your spouse will cherish even a short, simple note more than you can imagine.

Physical touch. Matthew 8 tells us a brief story in which a man with leprosy approaches Jesus. "If you are willing," he says, "You can make me clean." Jesus said, "I am willing, be clean," and touched the man, taking away his disease. It's a brief story—only three verses—and seems unremarkable. After all, Jesus healed many people. But there is one curious detail: Why did Jesus touch this man? We know from other healing accounts in the Gospels that Jesus didn't have to touch someone in order to heal them; He didn't even have to be in the same geographical area as the person He healed. Matthew's brief account doesn't tell us the reason for this divine touch, but consider what we know about leprosy in the ancient world: It was the most feared disease of all. People who were suspected of having leprosy were outcasts in every sense. In Jewish law, for instance, a leper had to live away from any town. They had to wear torn clothing, and cry out "Unclean!" as a warning to anyone who approached them. The man in Matthew 8 had not felt a human touch since the day he was diagnosed, which may have been years earlier. I believe Jesus touched the leper because He knew that this man needed emotional as well as physical healing. Touching him was an act of profound thoughtfulness.

Everyone needs physical contact with those who love them. But some people crave it more than others. If your spouse has this love language, you already know it. If you, on the other hand, don't really enjoy physical affection, this can be difficult. You want your space, but she keeps scooting closer. Understand that withholding affection from someone with this love language feels to them like intentional coldness. They wonder what they did wrong. On the other hand, every time you choose to initiate physical contact, it makes them feel loved. Taking her hand, giving him an unexpected hug or a passionate kiss, massaging her scalp as she drifts off to sleep…these are profound ways to communicate love to a person who craves them. PS: The love language of physical touch is not the same as our sex drive. Most men automatically think this is their love language because they enjoy sex. But when we do these things NOT expecting it to lead to something, then and only then it's an act of love.

Acts of service. John 13 contains the famous story of Jesus washing His disciples' feet. Preachers often emphasize the humility of Jesus, Lord of all Creation, doing a task so demeaning, it was considered beneath even a slave's dignity. But it was also a considerate act. Jesus wasn't just making a spiritual point; He was meeting a real need in the lives of His friends. This love language is hard for many of us to understand. When we think of love, we don't often think in terms of acts of service. Our romantic stories tell of lovers giving extravagant gifts, pouring out eloquent words of praise, or embracing one another passionately. As far as I know, there's no fairy tale in which the princess asks the dashing hero to plunge a stopped-up toilet. Yet Jesus did the ancient equivalent of that when He wanted to show His friends how important they were to Him.

People with this love language are doers. They can't walk away from an unfinished task. They may not respond to traditional romantic gestures the way we expect, but they are tireless in doing considerate, necessary things for those who love them. I know what I'm talking about; this is my wife's love language, whereas I'm a combination of words of affirmation and physical touch. Early in our marriage, I didn't appreciate all that she did for me. I just figured she liked living in a clean house. Actually, that is true. But once I realized that she wasn't working so hard simply for her benefit, I began to appreciate her acts of service more. In addition, I began to accept that fact that my wife appreciated action more than words. Today, I know that taking the initiative to clean up cat barf on our living room rug may be the most romantic thing I do all day. If your spouse has this love language, don't take him for granted. Mention the things he does. And find ways to serve him in return.

Quality time. Christians know that Jesus chose twelve disciples. It seems rather unfair, considering that He had hundreds of followers, that He would focus so much time and attention on a small group. Mark 3:14 tells us why He did this: *And he appointed twelve (whom he also named apostles) so that they might be with him and he might send them out to preach.* He was training these twelve people to carry on His mission once He was gone. But there was a more basic reason He chose the twelve: "So that they might be with Him." Jesus needed real friendship, which means time spent together. If He needed it, how much more do we?

If your spouse has this love language, she will often ask for undivided attention ("Please don't look at your phone when we're eating together" "Can we turn off the TV for a moment"). Superficial conversation is not enough for her. If she asks what you'd like to do, "Whatever you want" is not the right answer. If you make an effort to plan an experience together, or if you simply carve out time each day to be focused on her, that is a huge way to bless her. It comes down to this: How can you use your time to show her that nothing, other than God, matters more to you than she does?

Giving and receiving gifts. John 3:16 is arguably the most famous single verse in the entire Bible. You might say the Gospel is summed up in this one sentence: *For God so loved the world, He gave His only son, that whoever believes in Him should not perish but have eternal life.* At the heart of the Christian faith is not a creed, a ritual or a command…it's a gift. Our Lord is the ultimate gift, and He is also the ultimate gift-giver. He gave us life. When we trust in Him, He gives us new life. Someday, He'll give us a new home in Heaven. James 1:17 goes further than that. *Every good and perfect gift is from above, coming down from the Father of lights.* Any time you experience any good thing—a genuine laugh, a hug from a friend, a tasty meal—it's a gift from your Father, intended purely for your pleasure. It's Him saying, "I love you."

This love language, therefore, is not as selfish or materialistic as it sounds. Truth be told, people with the love language of gift-giving aren't concerned with the size or cost of the gift. A homemade present can be equally meaningful. If you understand their needs and desires well enough to come up with a thoughtful gift, they receive it as love. Of course, it takes time and focused attention to learn your spouse's needs and desires that well. It takes planning to be ready for special occasions. But that's just the point of this chapter: Your marriage is worth spending that time. Building something beautiful with your spouse is worth doing that work.

Learning how your spouse gives and receives love is a great place to start. But there is still more work to do...much more. The person you married is a deeply complex being. The longer you live together, the more you will learn about, say...

Her worst fear.
His deepest longing.
What sorts of people drive her up the wall.
The things you absolutely cannot say to him when he's in a bad mood.
The things that put him in a bad mood, to begin with.
What helps her unwind after a stressful day.
What he needs to hear you say, when the world has beaten him down.
How often she needs to see her parents.
How often he needs to get away from it all.

Learning your spouse's deepest emotional needs is every bit as important as learning their love language, and it takes much longer. It takes, in a sense, intense study. We need to study our spouse the way a marine biologist studies a bubble-tip anemone...the way an NFL quarterback studies a defense to get ready for a game...the way your dog studies that bite you're about to put in your mouth. Okay, that last one was a bad analogy, but you get the point.

What it boils down to is something I say every time I officiate a wedding: Love is a choice. We usually speak of love as an emotion. Being "in love" is indeed an emotion, and a powerful one. If you've ever been in love, you remember the intoxication of it. But emotion won't sustain a marriage. Love is a decision; it's an act of the will. Interestingly, the Bible never says Jesus likes us. Instead, it says *God demonstrates His love for us in that while we were still sinners, Christ died for us* (Romans 5:8). There was nothing in us that compelled Jesus to do this. He loved us when were wholly unlovely. And that love was more than sentiment. He met our deepest need–the need for redemption—not with words but with an action. He gave Himself up so we could live. That is love. Hallelujah! By the way, I am fairly certain Jesus does like you; after all, Ephesians 2:10 says you are His masterpiece, created for good works which He prepared ahead of time (my favorite verse). But it wasn't your sparkling intellect, your solid moral foundation, or your minty-fresh breath that led Jesus to die for you. He chose to do that, even though it wasn't in His best interests to do so.

Therefore I, as a Christian husband, should choose to learn how my wife receives love. I should choose to learn what her main emotional needs are. And I should choose to love her with actions that are intentionally chosen to make her feel loved, even if they go against my basic nature, and even if it's easier to just focus on my needs (it always is, by the way). This idea has helped me immensely in my own marriage. Now let me close this chapter out with two important thoughts:

Love the person you married, not the person you thought they'd be. My friend who I mentioned earlier had a pre-conceived idea: "Women love to get flowers." It was hard for him to accept that the woman he married needed her husband to be responsible, not just romantic. Here are some more examples:

A woman may not understand why her husband loves golf so much. But chances are, she knew that when she married him. Why did she expect him to magically change after "I do?"

A man may be baffled by his wife's dream of running a marathon. But if he loves her, he'll support that dream (he might even decide to run it with her).

She may not understand why he hates her flannel pajamas; you know, the super-comfortable ones that Grandma gave her, that button up to the chin. Why does he care what she wears to bed, after all? Well, he wants to find her attractive...and that should matter to her, too.

He may wish she enjoyed hanging out with his work friends. But she would rather spend time with people she trusts. Friendship and networking aren't the same for her, and he needs to recognize that.

Instead of trying to change your spouse's love language and emotional needs, accept them and choose to love them in those ways.

Don't focus on your needs. At times, you need to have a frank conversation with your spouse about a need of yours that isn't being fulfilled. There is a healthy way to have that conversation, and we'll talk about it later. However, your goal in marriage should be to think more often of your spouse's needs than your own. Time spent thinking of all the ways he disappoints you is wasted time. On the other hand, if you choose to meet his needs as best you can, chances are very good he will return the favor. Let me put it another way: I have seen a very direct correlation between the amount of time I spend thinking about my own needs and expectations, and my own unhappiness...and between my own joy and excitement in marriage and the amount of time I spend trying to meet her needs. Try it. It works!

But even if your spouse does her best to be everything you want her to be, she won't meet your needs perfectly. There is only One who can do that. And if she doesn't even try (which is possible, since you are in fact married to a sinner), there is One who loves you in a way no human spouse ever could. That love brings joy that outstrips the best and worst of any marriage. More on that in another chapter. Until then...choose to love.

Action Steps

1. Read *The Five Love Languages: The Secret to Love That Lasts,* by Gary Chapman. If you can get your spouse to read it with you, all the better. But even if it's just you reading the book, one person in a marriage who changes the way they love their spouse can change everything. If your spouse balks at reading a book with you, see if he/she will take the online love languages test at 5lovelanguages.com. Talk about what you learn about each other.

2. What do you know about your spouse that no one else knows (other than God and perhaps his/her parents)? Write out a list. Then spend the next month adding to that list.

3. Do an experiment on your spouse without telling them. Decide to do one thing per day to make them feel loved, and do it for ten days straight. Plan ahead, but be flexible. At the end of the ten days, how did you feel? How did your spouse respond?

Chapter 4

Marriage Wasn't Designed to Make you Happy

I had a friend who was single well into his late thirties. One day, an older man in our church said, "Son, you should get married! No man deserves to be free and happy his entire life!" We all laughed, because 1) The room was full of men, and 2) everyone knew the man speaking had been happily married for over fifty years, so it was truly a joke, not a comment spoken out of bitterness. The idea that marriage and happiness are mutually exclusive is a familiar comic trope ("Take my wife, please!" Rimshot!). But in the years since, I've known too many people stuck in unhappy marriages to find it funny anymore. It's soul-crushing to wake up day after day, realizing you are yoked to a relationship that sucks the happiness from your life. Often, you live with it, assuming this is how everyone's marriage is. But sometimes, you see a seemingly happy couple together, or you get a flash of memory to the days when you still had hope for your marriage, and the pain is intense. You can't help thinking, "I'd be so much happier if I weren't married anymore."

Despite what you've been told, marrying a Christian and being active in your faith actually DOES make your marriage stronger, and divorce less likely[1]. But it doesn't guarantee you'll be happy. Truth is, if you are a

---

[1] Ed Stetzer's article in Christianity Today, "Marriage, Divorce and the Church: What do the stats say, and can marriage be happy?" is available online and does a good job pulling together research on this subject. The gist of it is that simply being a member of a Christian church doesn't make

Christian who wants a happy marriage, I believe the first step is to realize that marriage was never designed to make you happy. That's a confusing sentence, I know. You can read it again, but it probably won't make any more sense the second time. So let me explain what I mean.

According to Genesis 2, the first marriage came about because God looked at the first man and said, *It is not good for the man to be alone. I will make a helper suitable for him* (Gen 2:18). By the way, that term "helper" doesn't imply any inferiority on the part of women, or that women exist to serve men (as a man, if that were what it meant, I'd be happy to tell you so!). The Hebrew term "helper" is most often used in the Old Testament to describe God Himself, after all (see Psalm 54:4 for an example). So how did God plan for men and women to help each other? Why did God create marriage in the first place?

I like the answer in Gary Thomas' book *Sacred Marriage*. The book is built around a single question: "What if God designed marriage to make us holy more than to make us happy?" Early in his book, Thomas tells of a conversation with his brother, who was single. Thomas told him, "If you want to become more like Jesus, I can't imagine any better thing to do than to get married. Being married forces you to face some character issues you'd never have to face otherwise." Thomas would say (and I now believe) marriage "helps" us by exposing the changes we still need to make in order to be the people God created us to be. Of all the marriage books I've ever read, *Sacred Marriage* may be the most important, specifically because it's not about how to be happier. It helps us see our marriage through God's eyes, and realize what He is trying to accomplish in our relationship. Let me give you an example of why this is so important.

Early in my marriage to Carrie, my anger was one of the big sources of our conflict. I had never really thought of myself as being an angry person. In fact, I was quite proud of my own patient nature; I hadn't been in a fistfight since I was twelve, and I was pretty good at putting up with difficult people, letting hurtful comments roll off my back. Of course, I did lose my temper at times, and my philosophy was that anger was like pressure in a valve; it needed to be released as harmlessly as possible. So I would occasionally flip out, scream and yell, throw things around, and be over it. In

---

you statistically more likely to have a strong, lasting marriage, but actively pursuing Christian faith does…by a lot.

many ways, that's how our culture teaches men to handle anger: Note how a baseball manager behaves when he disagrees with a call on the field, for instance. That was fine...until I got married. My wife is a gentle soul, and doesn't want to be around a person who acts like a raving lunatic. Of course, my moments of "pressure release" always happened at home, when my defenses were down and I didn't have to be on my best behavior. She hadn't really seen this side of me before marriage. This scenario would play out in our relationship: Something would set me off (the lawnmower wouldn't start, or Carrie would do or say something I found irritating) and I would blow my fuse. I would be over it in a few moments, and ready to move on. She would be angry at my outburst, and her method of handling anger was quite different from mine. Rather than screaming at me or throwing things, she would simply want to get away from me until she had gotten over it. This baffled me. Why didn't she let me express my anger once in a while? And why did it take her so long to get over being mad at me, when I was able to move on much more quickly? I would ask her these questions. Somehow the implication that my way of handling anger was better than hers didn't expedite reconciliation (shocking, I know). I would apologize, but that seemed more like a manipulation on my part than a sincere regretting of my actions. I would then get angry with her for not accepting my apology. And the cycle would continue. Rinse and repeat...that was the story of much of our early marriage.

Finally, it dawned on me. Maybe I DO have a problem with anger. Maybe there is a more mature way to deal with my frustrations. I began to notice how many Scriptures talk about patience, including James 1:19-20, *Everyone should be quick to listen, slow to speak, and slow to become angry. For man's anger does not produce the righteousness that God desires*. And Proverbs 29:11, *Fools give full vent to their anger; but a wise man calmly holds it back.* I also spent time around Christian men who were gentle and patient with their wives in situations that would have set me off. I began to think my philosophy on expressing anger was all wrong. I started to pray that God would teach me patience (I know people say never to ask God for that, but they are wrong. It was one of the best prayers I ever prayed). I started to consciously choose patience instead of anger in situations where I wanted to yell, wanted to throw things, wanted my wife to know just how angry I was. Guess what happened? Nothing. The pressure didn't build inside me to a bursting point. I didn't develop intestinal ulcers. Instead, I would hold my peace, and a few minutes later, I would realize how small and petty that source of irritation really was. Psychologists would perhaps say that I had re-conditioned my thinking. I had trained myself to react differently. But it wasn't me; it was the Holy Spirit, who used my marriage to show me a part of my character that I would never have dealt with otherwise.

Of course, my battle against anger wasn't over; there were more tests, especially once we began to have children. But I now knew that was a battle worth fighting, and I knew that with His help, it was a battle I could win. The point is that **God and my marriage teamed up to change my character** in a way I will always thank Him for. Let me say this a different way: In the early days of my marriage, I prayed often that God would make us happier, would bring peace to our relationship. I expected Him to simply make the conflict between us go away. But instead, He used the conflict between us to show me how I needed to change (I assume He did the same for her). I actually thank God now for those miserable days in our early twenties when we filled our small apartment with the toxic waste of our own immaturity, because without that, I never would have confronted my own sinfulness.

Eventually, Thomas' book helped me see this as the purpose of marriage. He didn't give me a wife just to make me happy; He gave me a wife so I could be holy (a word that means "set apart" for Him; the person He created me to be, a person who shows the world His glory). That means that tough times in our relationship are just as beneficial to me as the happy times, because it's through those struggles that I am forced to confront the parts of me that I want to ignore. Here's another way to say it: If God had revealed to me in some other way that I had a problem with anger–for instance, through a male friend taking me aside, or an employer sending me to anger management classes–I would not have taken it seriously. I hate to admit this, but I probably wouldn't have dealt with my anger simply because God wanted me to. But when I realized my marriage would happier if I did, it increased my motivation to do God's will. I would be making both God and my wife glad. That's what I mean when I say my marriage and God teamed up to change me. They continue to double-team me to this day, and I am grateful.

Let me be clear: I am not saying that, if you are in a desperately unhappy marriage, God is the cause of your unhappiness. He wasn't the cause of our fighting; our sin was. I am certainly not saying you should ever put up with abuse in your marriage (or any other relationship) in the hopes it will strengthen your character, or because you "deserve" it. That's a lie straight from the pit of Hell. If you read the Scriptures that talk about marriage, it's clear God meant that relationship to be a source of joy, comfort, and protection for us. He also meant it to be a profound picture of Divine love. My point is that loving another human being is the hardest thing we will ever do. It exposes our selfishness and our many other flaws. If your marriage isn't as happy as you think it should be, you're right…but the answer isn't to highlight all the ways you wish that parasite on the other side of the bed would change. The answer is to ask yourself, "What am I contributing to our unhappiness?" Let marriage do its work of exposing the parts of yourself that you've always ignored or rationalized away. Confront your sin in all its ugliness, and ask Him to help you become the person your spouse needs. Dedicate yourself to that task.

What if you began to grow so much in Christ, you were able to truly love this imperfect person you married, overlooking his flaws? What if the struggles of married life were far outweighed by the consistent joy and sense of purpose you felt each day? What if your spouse saw the change in you, and eventually decided to join you there? Marriage is a sacred thing, not just because God created it; not just because most people get married in a church; but because God can use it to change human lives. Give Him that chance.

Action Steps

1. If you are married, what sins has your marriage exposed in you? Here's another way to answer that question: "If I were more _____ and/or less _____, I know our marriage would be better." Take those sins to God in prayer. Ask Him to show you how to change.

2. If you're not yet married, pray and ask God to show you the answer to this question: "What sins, bad habits and personality quirks are most likely to create problems for me when I get married?"

3. Address these issues head-on. That may mean seeking treatment for addictions, seeing a counselor regularly, or ridding your life of bad influences. It will definitely take work on your part. The Bible describes the process of changing for the better (spiritual growth) as requiring two participants—God and you. See Philippians 2:12-13. We are called up on to "work out" our salvation. That doesn't mean we save ourselves. It means we work to make our salvation in Christ evident in every area of our lives.

But we can't do it alone. *It is God who works in you...* So pray about the ways you need to change, then work like your life depends on it. Do not, under any circumstances, allow yourself to stop growing.

   4. Consider reading *Sacred Marriage*, by Gary Thomas. He takes this topic much deeper than I can in just a few paragraphs. I believe it will change the way you look at your marriage.

Chapter 5

Sex Is Not Simple

      At the start of this book, I confessed that I am not a marriage expert. Now, let me add another caveat: I am also not a sex expert (Would that be a "sexpert"? Never mind). I do not claim to know the sure-fire steps guaranteed to give you a smoldering sexual relationship with your spouse. But, like many of you, I grew up in the wake of the sexual revolution of the 1960s. That means that in my lifetime, I have heard a ton of different messages about sex: From friends in locker rooms, teachers in health class, depictions of it in TV and movies, articles about it in magazines, and sermons and Bible studies at church. Even many of our advertisements sell particular messages about sexuality. In the past twenty years, the presence of the internet has increased the number of these messages we hear each day exponentially. Many of the messages we hear about sex—even some we get from Christian sources—don't agree with the ancient wisdom found in the Bible. In this chapter, I want to highlight three main categories of disagreement between popular culture and Scripture on the subject of sex. And I want to share the myth about sex that I believed before I got married.

Message #1: Religion is sexually repressive.
Several years ago, I was part of a discussion on an internet message board. I don't remember what the main topic was, but I perked up when one member of our discussion confidently wrote, "Christianity teaches that sex is for reproduction only, not for pleasure. So you can only have sex when you're actively trying to have kids." I replied, "I have read the Bible several times, and I am not aware of that teaching anywhere in it. And if you know

where it is, please don't tell my wife!" He did not respond. I wonder where he got that idea from? Perhaps he was confused by Roman Catholic teaching that contraception is immoral (A teaching, by the way, which comes from Church tradition, not from any direct reading of Scripture). Regardless, his statement is indicative of a prevalent belief in society: The more religious you are, the less likely you will be to have a satisfying sex life. This is because God considers sex something dirty, which we must never talk about or think about. When a husband and wife want to have children, they may do it, but quickly, with all the lights off, making sure not to enjoy themselves. And if they're Baptists, they must never do it standing up…that might lead to dancing.

That last sentence was a joke, by the way.

Actually, when people read the Bible for the first time, they are often surprised at how frank, even earthy, the Bible is in talking about sex. For instance, here's a good trivia question for you: What is the first command in Scripture? Answer: *Be fruitful and multiply* (Genesis 1:28). Think about that for a moment. What do humans do in order to multiply? It's okay, you can say it out loud. That's right, the first command God ever gave to a human being was to tell a husband and wife to have sex. Often.

That's not all. Far from teaching that sex is only for reproduction, several passages urge us to enjoy our physical relationship with our spouse. Proverbs 5:18-19, for instance, advises husbands to stay faithful to their wives with these words: *May your fountain be blessed, and may you rejoice in the wife of your youth. A loving doe, a graceful deer, may her breasts satisfy you always; may you ever be captivated by her love.* There is not room here to quote the entire Song of Solomon, but let me sum it up for you: This is an entire book of the Bible dedicated to describing the erotic relationship between a husband and wife. So when a husband and wife take pleasure in each other's bodies, they are actually obeying God. Fulfilling sex within marriage pleases the One who created us.

Here's one more interesting command from Scripture: 1 Corinthians 7:3-4 reads, *The husband should fulfill his marital duty to his wife, and likewise the wife to her husband. The wife's body does not belong to her alone but also to her husband. In the same way, the husband's body does not belong to him alone but also to his wife. Do not deprive one another except by mutual consent and for a time, so that you may devote yourself to prayer.* Just to be clear: That command should be read in the context of love. Love does not force itself on anyone, and I must never use the Bible to coerce my wife (physically or emotionally) to do what she doesn't want to do. What it does show is that God wants married people to prioritize fulfilling their spouse's sexual needs as part of a healthy love relationship.

You might respond, "But the Bible clearly teaches that sex, with all of its pleasures, is only permitted within heterosexual married relationships. Isn't that repressive?" I will talk more about this in my third point below. But for now, I will share this story from Atlanta pastor Andy Stanley: A young woman who had been visiting his church spoke to him one day, saying that she liked many things about Jesus and His teachings, but she couldn't accept Christian beliefs on sexuality. Why would God forbid so many people to experience something so pleasurable? Stanley responded by asking her a question of his own: "Has sex outside of marriage made your life better, or more complicated?" I think that's a question our entire culture must confront. Sixty years ago, the Sexual Revolution promised us that if we threw off the shackles of sexual regulations imposed by authorities like religion, we would be happier for it. Has that come true? I can think of several ways our society is healthier now than in 1960: Civil rights, for one. But are marriages healthier and more fulfilling today? Are families more likely to stick together? Are there fewer broken hearts, leading to lower rates of addiction, despair, and suicide attempts? I think we would all agree that in those metrics, we are worse today than before. What if the "restrictions" imposed by the Bible are more like the rules that govern other areas of life? For instance, you can drive the wrong way on a freeway, eat a steak that's been sitting at room temperature for a day, and dive head-first into a shallow pool if you want. You may even get away with it. But eventually, you'll get hurt. These rules don't restrict us; they give us freedom to enjoy a car trip, a steak dinner, and a refreshing swim. God created sex. He created it for our pleasure. And He told us how to enjoy it. Calling His guidelines "repressive" is the height of arrogance and foolishness.

Message #2: Sex is no big deal.

A friend once said something I've never been able to get out of my head: "You Christians are always mad, mostly because you're afraid somebody, somewhere might be having fun." I hate to admit it, but I knew exactly what he was talking about. Throughout history, we find examples of Christians preaching against—even legislating against—stuff other people do for fun:

Dancing, drinking, playing cards, going to the movies, and having sex…oh yes, we love to control people's sexual choices. We shame those who step out of line, never letting them forget it. We elevate sexual sins as if they matter more to God than all other categories of sin. The world responds with a collective shrug: "Why do you make such a big deal about sex? It's just an exchange of bodily fluids. It's just two people doing what comes naturally."

It's interesting to note how many times Jesus came into contact with people who were seen as "dirty" because they had fallen short of God's standards when it came to sexuality. In every case—whether He was stopping an accused adulteress from being stoned to death by an angry mob, forgiving a "sinful woman" who had tearfully anointed Him with costly oil, or responding to charges that He was a friend of prostitutes—Jesus gave them dignity. He showed them grace. He restored them instead of consigning them to life's dustbin. Over the last two thousand years, the followers of Jesus have often treated sexual sins as unforgivable, but Jesus never did…and never will.

On the other hand, Scripture clearly teaches that sex IS a big deal. Note 1 Corinthians 6:18-20: *Flee from sexual immorality. All other sins a person commits are outside the body, but whoever sins sexually, sins against their own body. Do you not know that your bodies are temples of the Holy Spirit, who is in you, whom you have received from God? You are not your own; you were bought at a price. Therefore honor God with your bodies.*

Paul wasn't saying that sinning sexually changes how God feels about us. But he was saying it affects us differently than other sins. Sex is more than the fulfilling of a physical desire, like eating or sleeping. Something happens in the act of sex that doesn't happen anywhere else. Deep down, we all know this to be true. Why else are the criminal penalties for rape different from those for simple assault? Because we all acknowledge that a person who has been violated sexually faces a different type of trauma than someone who has bruises or perhaps a broken bone. The body heals, but when we rob someone of the right to share that intimate act willingly, lovingly, we have wounded their soul. If that is true when sex is forcibly taken, it is also true when it is casually given away. God made our bodies for certain purposes. When we use our bodies in ways they were never designed to be used, there are consequences.

Jesus famously said in Matthew 5:27-28, *You have heard that it was said, 'You shall not commit adultery.' But I tell you that anyone who looks at a woman lustfully has already committed adultery with her in his heart.* I need to point out three things about that command: First, the responsibility is on men to govern how they look at women, not on women to avoid tempting men. There is a place for a discussion of modesty, but that's not what Jesus is talking about here. Religious movements that put the onus of responsibility on women, who treat women as if their bodies are shameful, who legislate what clothes women are allowed to wear, are not operating in the Spirit of Christ. Jesus didn't tell women to wrap themselves in burlap from nose to toes; He told men to take responsibility for their eyes and thoughts.

Second, this command shows how seriously God takes our sexual thoughts. Thanks to internet technology, a person no longer needs to drive to a seedy adult bookstore to purchase pornography. It's available on our phones! In this hyper-sexualized culture, Christ's words seem ridiculously out of date. You may be wondering what defines "lust" in His eyes. It's not sinful to notice an attractive person. That would be impossible to avoid. God created us to notice those things; otherwise, men and women would never get together! I can notice that a woman is attractive, and still treat her as I would a sister or a daughter. But if I try to capture her in my mind, using her beauty for my own gratification, then it's lust. God knows that the way I see another person determines how I will treat her. I am called to love my neighbor as myself. Choosing to treat every woman with the respect she is due as a daughter of the King, instead of focusing on her physical form, is essential for loving her as I should.

Third, think of the terrible evils that could have been avoided if men had obeyed this one command. In 2017, the #MeToo movement became a cultural phenomenon. Famous men in the worlds of entertainment, business, politics and organized religion were exposed and dethroned at such a rapid rate, the 24-hour news cycle struggled to keep up. Yet think of the women who endured abuse at the hands of these men…and how many exponentially more women endured similar pain from non-famous men. And all of it—every single incidence—was a result of men treating women in a way that contradicted the words of Jesus. Sex IS a big deal, period.

Message #3: Sex is the ultimate thing.

"Wait," you might be saying, "I thought the world believed sex was no big deal. Now you say the world believes sex is the ultimate thing. Which is it?" I never said the world is consistent in its messaging. I'm sure we can all agree that sex is presented to us in popular media as the highest of all human experiences. People today are seeking the sublime, an encounter that will lift them far above the petty concerns of everyday life. In ages past, we satisfied that urge by communing with God. But in an era when most people don't trust organized religion, we settle for the next best thing: Really great sex. I wouldn't have the first clue what percentage of people actually experience this transcendent sex that the commercials, pop songs and gas station romance novels promise us. But everyone seems to be chasing it. And why not? If it's the summit of human pleasure, how could I possibly be happy without it?

This helps explain why debates over sexual issues, such as the definition of marriage, are such a cultural battleground. If sexual fulfillment brings ultimate happiness, then it is an inalienable right. How can someone deny us the right to pursue that fulfillment with any consenting adult we choose? In fact, our pursuit of that fulfillment should not be simply allowed; it must be celebrated. Any person or group who disapproves of our choices obviously hates us, and must therefore be exposed as evil. It's interesting, isn't it? For centuries, certain segments of organized religion treated sexual sin as the ultimate sin. Today, secular society has created its own form of fundamentalism, in which sex is seen as the ultimate good, and anyone who disagrees is treated as a heretic.

In a strange way, Christian churches sell their own version of this message. Notice that the ministries of most churches are focused on married couples and parents. Single adults have a hard time finding their place. If you're single and older than your mid-twenties, you've probably lost count of the number of times someone in church has asked you, in one way or another, "When are you getting married?" The obvious implication is that you couldn't possibly live a full and meaningful life within a celibate life.

Yet Jesus was a lifelong celibate man, and He lived the fullest, most meaningful life in human history. The Apostle Paul, also, was unmarried. In 1 Corinthians 7, he wrote to tell young Christians that marriage was a good thing. But in verses 6 and 7, he adds this interesting caveat: *I say this as a concession, not as a command. I wish that all of you were as I am. But each of you has your own gift from God; one has this gift, another has that.* Paul wasn't singing the words of the Queen song, "Can anybody find me somebody to love?" He actually considered his singleness a gift!

So no, sex is not the ultimate thing. Remember that line at the end of *Jerry Maguire*, when Jerry says to Dorothy, "You complete me"? It's a great line. But it's baloney. Only the God who created you can complete you. No human being, no sexual experience, can do that.

The Myth I believed: Sex Comes Naturally

In the first chapter, I mentioned the Christian-Marital Industrial Complex that was so prevalent in my young adulthood. I came of age in a time when preachers were just beginning to talk about sex from the pulpit. And they wanted boys like me to know that if I would turn my raging hormones over to the Lord, I would be glad I had, once I got married. I didn't actually hear WA Criswell's "Wheelbarrow Sermon" (Again, see chapter one), but I heard versions of it. I truly believed that if my fiancé and I remained sexually abstinent until our wedding night, spectacular sex would be automatic. I combined that with the lessons about sex I had gleaned from PG-13 movies: The sex drives of men and women are always the same. A woman is always thrilled to get lingerie as a gift. And sex is always spontaneous, passionate and exciting. In my mind, sex was going to be simple and wonderful. I couldn't wait.

Let me be clear about two things: One, I have absolutely zero regrets about not "sowing my wild oats" before I got married. My wife and I share something that neither of us has ever shared with anyone else, and that's amazing. And two, sex is indeed wonderful. But simple? Nope. Without going into detail (I just pictured you, the reader, whispering, "O, thank God!"), it took us a while to get good at this. We—two healthy young adults who were ridiculously attracted to each other, had to work at this part of our marriage…the one part I thought would take care of itself. And I know we're not the only ones. Sad to say, plenty of married couples never get this right. Even sadder, plenty of married couples settle for what they have, instead of striving for more.

Again, I don't have any tips. What works for us probably wouldn't work for you anyway. I just know that one day in my middle years, I realized that our sexual relationship was way more satisfying after more than two decades of marriage than it was the first year we got married. Twenty-two year old me would never have believed that, but it's true. How did it happen? It happened because we prioritized it. It happened because we prayed for it. It happened because we communicated with each other. It happened because we learned to understand and accept each other's rhythms, desires, and turn-offs. It happened because—let's be honest—we adjusted our expectations. It happened because we learned to focus on pleasing each other instead of trying to satisfy ourselves. In other words, we came to "know" one another, in the biblical sense of that word. That takes time, effort, and honesty. For you, it may take more than just those things. Some couples have physical or emotional issues that require professional treatment. You may be embarrassed to seek help in your sexual relationship with your spouse, but I urge you to overcome it. This is worth the work.

There's something else I've been meaning to address, and this seems as good a place as any: Women sometimes worry, "What if my husband stops finding me attractive someday?" Women—especially Christian women steeped in the Christian-Marital Industrial Complex and its culture of sexual purity—have been told again and again that "men are visual." As a man, I can testify that it's true. But I have good news for you: You. Are. His. Type. You don't have to compete with supermodels or scantily-clad MTV vixens for your husband's attractions. He doesn't expect you to look like what he sees on the screen. How do I know you are his type? Because he married you. You see, men are not complex creatures. A woman may fall passionately in love with a man who is miles from her physical ideal because of any number of attributes. But I've never met a man who fell in love with a woman who he found physically unattractive. That doesn't mean your looks are the most important thing to him. But it does mean he liked what he saw when he first saw you. So…not to put too fine a point on it, but…whatever you did to attract him back then, as long as you (at least occasionally) keep doing that, he'll be a happy man. To clarify: Your husband has to live in the real world. You will change your hairstyle from time to time, even though he protests. Your appearance will change in other ways as the years roll on, no matter what you do. Just don't stop trying to attract him. He'll be thankful for it.

Now, to men: If you read that last paragraph, you may have noticed the third-from-last sentence: "Your appearance will change…as the years roll on, no matter what you do." This is true. It will happen, and you'd better get ready for it. I heard someone say once, "Most problems in marriage happen because the wife thought her husband would change once they got married, and the husband thought his wife never would." There is a lot of truth in that, especially on the male side. So let me put this in extremely frank terms: If you love your wife's body, start praying now…because it won't always look that way. If she gets pregnant, you may struggle internally as you see that body change rapidly. But—and I can't say this strongly enough—she doesn't need to know you're having those struggles! Pray that God would help you to find her just as attractive as her body changes. Pray that you would always be kind in what you say to her about her appearance. The same goes for whatever might be your favorite physical feature of your wife. Take a look at the pictures of your parents on their wedding day. What happened to them will happen to both of you. So pray now, consistently and sincerely, that you will learn to find your wife beautiful no matter what.

Action Steps

1. If you're not married, pray and ask God to help you live a joyfully celibate life until and unless you get married. If you're having a difficult time maintaining that standard, tell Him about it and ask Him to provide the help and support you need. Pray that, if marriage is in your future, He would prepare you to meet the sexual needs of your spouse, and to be faithful in every way to him/her. Make this part of your regular prayer life.

2. If you are married, resist the temptation to "settle" in your sexual relationship with your spouse. Pray about it. Communicate honestly—but gently—about it. If you're the "unhappy" partner, ask God to change YOUR heart, not your spouse's; in other words, to help you love them even if you never get the fulfillment you wish you had. On the other hand, if you're hearing complaints from your spouse in this area, take them seriously. What would help you be more willing? Do you need more sleep? Would a weekly date night help? Is there some habit of your spouse's that is turning you off? Do you need to see a doctor about your lack of desire? You may be tempted to write this off, to think, "We're not newlyweds. He/she needs to accept that this is the way it is." Frankly, if that happens, it will be terrible for your marriage. It will mean your spouse has given up. So prioritize this.

Chapter 6

Competition is a Curse

It was around twelve years ago, but I can still picture it vividly. I had just stepped behind the pulpit to preach, as I do every Sunday, when I spotted someone in the pews who I recognized immediately: It was Case Keenum, the quarterback of my favorite college football team, the University of Houston Cougars. I felt a little flutter in my stomach. I literally said these words in my head: "Alright, Berger. I hope you brought your A-game today." My wife and Carrie and I actually became friends of Case and his soon-to-be wife Kimberly shortly after that, although it had more to do with our mutual friend and UH chaplain Mikado Hinson than it did my preaching. Eventually, Case moved on to the NFL, and now we see them only from afar, but he will always be my favorite athlete of all time. Why? First of all, because he's a true man of God. If you're a sports fan, check out his book, *Playing for More*. If you know someone who is, get them a copy. Seriously. What he writes in that book is what he lives.

But the second thing I admire about Case is his intense competitive nature. Case grew up in Abilene, in West Texas. When he was a senior in high school, he led his team on a last-minute touchdown drive to win the state championship over Cuero, which incidentally was my high school's arch-rival. Still, UH was literally the only college program to offer Case a scholarship. He was considered too small to play quarterback on that level. By the time he graduated, Case had thrown for more passing yards, touchdowns and completions than any quarterback in college football history. Again, the "experts" on the next level made the same mistake: Not a single NFL team drafted Case. Yet he has outlasted most of the highly-rated quarterbacks who were drafted ahead of him, and has completed nine seasons in the NFL. If you want to see something amazing—even if you aren't a football fan—google "Minneapolis Miracle" and watch his most famous moment. You can thank me later.

So I love sports. I especially love athletes who overcome a lack of size or overwhelming talent through a sheer will to win. But what works on playing fields—or classrooms, dance studios, concert halls and boardrooms—can be absolutely fatal to a marriage. Competition between spouses is a curse.

I learned this in our first year of marriage. As I mentioned earlier, we fought a lot that first year. This was a surprise to me, since neither of us were particularly confrontational in our relationships with others. One day as I was analyzing our problem, I realized the irony: Our fights were always over inconsequential things. For instance, one night we had a long, intense argument over how to fold towels. In the middle of the argument—literally as I was yelling at her—I had this thought run through my head: "Why are you fighting about this? You don't care how the towels get folded." Then I answered my own question, internally: "We do everything her way. I want us to do something my way, even if it's something stupid like the way we fold towels." Again, this entire internal dialogue took place while I was yelling at my wife. Don't tell me men can't multi-task! Wait, that's not my point…

My problem was that I wanted to win. I wanted things to go my way, even things that weren't important. And I'm not the only one. If you're married, you may recognize the following signs of an over-competitive marriage relationship (and no, I haven't been spying on you):

We guilt-trip and compare: "I'll bet I'm the only woman on earth who has to put up with this." "John's wife doesn't complain about him hunting. It must be nice."

We keep score: "I've cleaned the kitchen the last three nights by myself. It's your turn." "Why would I go to your parents' house with you? You didn't go to mine last week."

We strategize: "If I ask her while the kids are up, she's more likely to say yes. She doesn't want to fight in front of them." "Next time he pulls that little stunt on me, here's what I'm going to do. That'll teach him."

We manipulate with words like "never" and "always." "You never listen to me." "We always end up doing what you want on the weekends."

We threaten: "Say that one more time. I dare you. I double-dog dare you." (When you're quoting *Pulp Fiction* to your spouse, it's rarely a good sign).

Please understand—I am not saying we can never disagree with our spouse, or point out their flaws, or ask them to change. In our next chapter, I'll talk about how to do that in a way that builds our marriage. Competition within marriage, however, tears it down.

God told us it would be this way. In Genesis 3, we read about an event theologians call The Fall of Man. The first man and woman, Adam and Eve, lived in a world without sin, in perfect harmony with God and each other. Then they chose to separate from God, to do things their own way. In Genesis 3, God explained to Adam and Eve that their decision had warped the fabric of Creation. When sin entered a sinless world, it brought with it all sorts of terrible consequences. Human work would be frustrating and fruitless. Children would be born only after a time of intense pain and danger. And most of all, death would be a reality for us all. But God also told Eve about how sin would affect her relationship with her husband: *Your desire shall be contrary to your husband, but he shall rule over you* (Genesis 3:16).

This is a highly controversial and often-misunderstood sentence, so let's clear a couple things up: First, the word "desire" has nothing to do with sexual desire. It refers to a desire to dominate. In the very next chapter, God speaks to Cain, who is angry with his brother Abel, saying, *Sin is crouching at your door. Its desire is contrary to you, but you must rule over it* (Genesis 3:7). So God pictures sin like an animal preparing to pounce on its potential victim, using this same word "desire." Second, when God tells Eve that her husband shall rule over her, he isn't saying that husbands should be the unquestioned ruler of their homes. I realize that has sometimes been taught in churches, but it isn't what God is saying. This isn't a command, it's a curse. He's saying, "In your marriage, you'll both want to win. You'll want to dominate him, to get your way. Since he's physically stronger, he'll dominate you. And it's all because of sin." He's talking about the curse of competition. In case you don't believe I'm right in this interpretation, apply that logic to the other consequences God tells Adam and Eve about: When He tells Eve that childbirth will be difficult and painful, is that a command or a curse? If it's a command, then it's a sin for us to do anything to relieve a woman's pain in childbirth. When he tells Adam his work in the fields will be difficult, is that a command or a curse? If it's a command, then it's a sin for us to use modern technology to make cultivating crops easier and more fruitful. Is that how we think? Of course not. We are grateful when we find a way to improve life in this cursed world. We should be especially glad for any help we can get in overcoming the competitive curse in our marriage.

Surprisingly, we find the answer in another controversial and often-misunderstood passage of Scripture: Ephesians 5:22-33. True story: I did my first wedding ceremony in my hometown before I had become pastor of a church, and I used this passage as my text. Afterward, a young woman who I had grown up with approached me. She said, and I quote: "You did a good job explaining that text. I still don't like it." So with that as our introduction:

22 Wives, submit to your own husbands, as to the Lord. 23 For the husband is the head of the wife even as Christ is the head of the church, his body, and is himself its Savior. 24 Now as the church submits to Christ, so also wives should submit in everything to their husbands.

25 Husbands, love your wives, as Christ loved the church and gave himself up for her, 26 that he might sanctify her, having cleansed her by the washing of water with the word, 27 so that he might present the church to himself in splendor, without spot or wrinkle or any such thing, that she might be holy and without blemish.[a] 28 In the same way husbands should love their wives as their own bodies. He who loves his wife loves himself. 29 For no one ever hated his own flesh, but nourishes and cherishes it, just as Christ does the church, 30 because we are members of his body. 31 "Therefore a man shall leave his father and mother and hold fast to his wife, and the two shall become one flesh." 32 This mystery is profound, and I am saying that it refers to Christ and the church. 33 However, let each one of you love his wife as himself, and let the wife see that she respects her husband.

If you're unfamiliar with this passage, and especially if you are a woman, you may feel like my classmate was right. And I fully admit this passage (along with Genesis 3:16 and a handful of other passages) has been misused by preachers in the past to prop up the unbiblical idea that men should always be in charge, and women are, at best, their cheerleaders. It has even been tragically misused to tell abused women to "submit" to their abusers. Taken out of context, it's easy to see how these kinds of teachings could come from this passage. But that is absolutely not what Paul is saying. To understand what Paul meant, and how to overcome the competitive instinct in our marriage, we need to answer these three questions:

What does it mean to submit? In the sport of Mixed-Martial Arts, competitors sometimes employ "submission moves," in which they force their opponent's body into a position so uncomfortable, the opponent is compelled to "tap out," or give up the match. This is how we often view the idea of submission in our relationships. It's saying, "Alright, you win." But that's not the biblical idea of submission. Jesus submitted to God the Father (John 5:19, 6:38, 12:50). Think about that. Jesus created everything that exists (John 1:1-14). He is fully God, co-equal with the Father (John 10:30, Colossians 2:9, Romans 9:5, among many others).[2] Yet Jesus chose to submit to the Father. It wasn't because He was inferior in some way. He wasn't "giving in" to someone who had defeated Him. He was saying, "I'm not in competition with my Father. I am following His plan, not my own." Jesus did this willingly, joyfully. And the result was our salvation.

In relationships, submission means saying, "I am going to override my competitive instincts. I'm going to put you ahead of me. Instead of trying to bend you to my will, I am going to do what is best for our relationship." I read about a couple who had been married for fifty years. At the celebration, someone asked the husband, "Do you have any advice for how to stay married so long?" "Yeah," the husband said, "Never win a fight." When I tell that story, people often laugh. They think I'm recycling the old trope that says the two most important words for a husband to know are "Yes, dear." But that's not what that story means to me. Submission doesn't mean you always agree with the other person. It does mean that you always do what is best for your relationship, instead of doing what is best for you. It means we counteract the old curse, in which husbands seek to dominate their wives, and wives seek to manipulate their husbands. It means, in the end, our goal is not to force our partner to say, "Alright, you win," but to find a way that both of us can say, "We won."

---

[2] This isn't the time or place for us to discuss how it's possible for Jesus to be both fully man and fully God, or that Father, Son and Holy Spirit are one God, but three separate persons. But that is unquestionably the teaching of Scripture.

Why is the command for husbands different than it is for wives? Actually, it's not. Notice verse 21, the verse that leads into our passage about marriage:

>...*submitting to one another out of reverence for Christ.*

Remember, Paul and the other biblical writers did not put verse numbers in their writing. Those were added centuries later. So in Paul's text, he didn't pause between verses 21 and 22. Nor did he actually write the word, "submit" in verse 22. That is supplied by English translators for the sake of clarity. Here's what he literally wrote:

>...*submitting to one another out of reverence for Christ, wives to your husbands as to the Lord.*

Paul is saying that we should practice submission in all our relationships. Then, as a way of providing an example, he commands wives to practice that principle toward their husbands. Then, in verse 25, he commands husbands to love their wives like Christ loved the church. In case we think of "love" as a sentimental feeling, he reminds us that Christ's love for His Bride was fully displayed when He died for us. Instead of giving husbands a different, less sacrificial command, he raises the bar of submission to the example of Jesus Himself.

It's hard for us to comprehend how revolutionary this teaching was when Paul wrote it. In the Roman world of the first century, men held all the cultural power. In Roman weddings, "It was traditional on the wedding day to declare to the bride that when her husband committed adultery with a prostitute or a woman of easy virtue, it was not a sign that he did not love her, but simply a way of gratifying his passions."[3] To men living in a culture where wives were seen as domestic help at best, Paul said, "Every day, you need to lay down your rights for her sake."

For the women who first read Paul's words in the first century, submission was already a way of life. But coming to Christ had brought them a new status. They were now members of a Kingdom in which *There is neither Jew nor Greek, there is neither slave nor free, there is no male and female, for you are all one in Christ Jesus* (Galatians 3:28). They followed a Savior who treated women with dignity and respect, who chose a woman (Mary

---

[3] Winter, B. (1994). 1 Corinthians. In D. A. Carson, R. T. France, J. A. Motyer, & G. J. Wenham (Eds.), *New Bible commentary: 21st century edition* (4th ed., p. 1171). Leicester, England; Downers Grove, IL: Inter-Varsity Press.

Magdalene) to be the first eyewitness of the resurrection, the most important single act in history. These women may have been tempted to think, therefore, that their newfound commitment to Jesus made their marital bonds obsolete. But Paul says that, instead, submitting to their husbands was a way of loving Jesus. He ends the entire passage by commanding wives to respect their husbands. In my opinion, some teachers have made too much of the distinction between love and respect ("Women need love, but men need respect," they say, as if we don't all need both). But I think Paul is being very intentional here. A man who did what Paul was commanding here was putting himself in a vulnerable position. He was forfeiting the right that human societies have, for centuries, told him he naturally has: The right to dominate his wife. The wife could, therefore, take full advantage of the situation, treating him with scorn. This often, in fact, happens. I sometimes say, "Ladies, if you can't talk about your husband without rolling your eyes, you need to repent." There is always laughter, but usually the nervous sort. Instead, wives need to realize that they, more than any other human on earth, hold their husband's self-image in their hands. You can treat him like a spineless loser or an incorrigible child, and he's likely to live up to that image. But if you treat him like a hero instead, even if (especially if!) he doesn't deserve it, watch what happens…

What does it mean that the husband is the head? Bible scholars fall into two different camps when it comes to male/female relations in Scripture. Complementarians believe that, while men and women are equally loved and important in God's sight, He has created them to play different roles within the family and the Church. Their roles "complement" each other, but are not the same. Egalitarians, on the other hand, believe there is no distinction in God's eyes between the roles men and women can play. Complementarians view verse 23 as proof that God wants men to be the unquestioned leaders of their homes. A family cannot be everything it was called to be, they say, unless the husband and father steps up and fulfills his role. Egalitarians, on the other hand, say that Paul is simply making an analogy, and that this should not indicate any distinction in roles between men and women. They point to verse 25 as proof that the only way a husband is like Jesus is in the command to lay down his life for his bride. Therefore, they would say, husbands are not superior in rank to their wives, but are called to sacrifice for them.

Now, I'm going to make both groups mad.

I believe the complementarians are right to say that husbands are called to a unique role within marriage. Nowhere in Scripture are wives called to function as the head of their husbands, but here in verse 23, we have a clear command for husbands to fulfill that function to their wives. But I believe the egalitarians are correct to say this headship doesn't mean that husbands "outrank" their wives. Think about the relationship of Christ to His Bride. He never forced anyone to follow Him. His every action toward us was motivated by love. He came *not to be served, but to serve, and give His life as a ransom for many* (Matthew 20:28). He was fully God, but didn't stalk around insisting we treat Him as God, instead He *emptied Himself, taking the form of a servant...He humbled Himself by becoming obedient to the point of death, even death on a cross.*

What does it mean that God sees me as the head of my wife? It doesn't mean I get "the last word" on everything (as much as I wish it did!). Nowhere in Scripture are husbands told to command their wives to submit. Any husband who tries that is a fool, in the most biblical sense of the word. It also doesn't mean that I as the husband must make all the decisions. After almost three decades of marriage, I have learned that while I am certainly stronger than my wife in some areas, she has more expertise in others. If I'm smart, I'll defer to her judgment in the areas where she knows more than I. Instead, my headship is a matter of responsibility, not privilege. Just as Jesus chose to take responsibility for His Bride by dying for her, so I am called to take responsibility for my wife and children. Someday, I will stand before the Lord Himself. Though I am saved fully by His grace, I will still give an account for my life. I believe part of that judgment will revolve around what kind of husband and father I was. I cannot ultimately guarantee my wife and children will follow the Lord, anymore than Jesus could guarantee that all of us would believe in Him. But I will be judged on whether I did all I could to help them become what God in His wisdom created them to be.

The reason I see headship in this way is because of verses 26-27. Jesus doesn't just want to give us a ticket to Heaven. The Gospel is redemption. It's about changing us from our sinful selves into the perfect image of His righteousness. Jesus, the Head of the Church, is constantly working to make us into the people He created us to be. So, for me to be a Christlike head of my family, I will need to be working alongside Him in recreating my wife and kids. That means I pray for them daily. I make time to disciple them, including active involvement in a local church. And most of all, I live out my faith before them in an authentic, compelling way. It means that every husband is the most important pastor that his family will ever have, and that role is the most important role he can possibly fill.

This is a beautiful image that, if you stop and let it sink in, can change everything about marriage for you. Some people think they've married the perfect person and say to themselves, "As long as she never changes, I'll be happy." But their spouse inevitably changes, because that's what happens. And they are left profoundly disappointed. Others marry, thinking, "I've found someone with the potential to be everything I want him to be, as long as he lets me mold him to my will." Inevitably, that results in devastating conflict, because no one likes being manipulated like that. But if you heed verses 26-27, whether you are a man or a woman, you start to see your spouse not in terms of how they meet your needs in the present time, or how they *could* meet your needs if they changed, but in terms of who God is making them into. You start to see, "God created my spouse with an incredible purpose in the world. And I get to be part of helping them become that person He is making them into, helping them fulfill that purpose. And when that happens, oh, the difference he will make in the lives of so many! Oh, the glory that God will get in seeing her use her gifts!" When we think that way, we lay down our own desires to cooperate with God in this incredible building project that is discipleship. And, in a sneaky way, we end up happier in our marriage, too!

But in verse 32, Paul shows us the stakes are much higher than simply our own marital happiness: *This mystery is profound, and I am saying it refers to Christ and the Church.* Paul is saying that, ultimately, human marriage was created to be more than a source of earthly companionship and procreation. It is a picture of the relationship between Jesus and His people. After all, when Christ spoke about His Second Coming, He often compared it to a wedding feast. Think about that. In the same way a bridegroom yearns to be with his bride, so Jesus cannot wait to be finally, fully united with us. And just like a wedding feast in first-century Israel was the height of celebration (the best food and wine, reunions with friends and loved ones long missed, music, dancing, laughter…), so the coming Kingdom of God, The New Earth, will be a place of joy like nothing we've ever seen. If you're ever worried that Heaven will be boring, remember these two facts: The One who created all things, including everything you consider "fun," is excited to spend eternity with you. And He compares that time not to a church service, but a celebration.

All of that means when we stop competing with our spouse and consistently start putting them ahead of ourselves, we won't just be happier (although we will definitely be that too). We'll be a walking billboard advertising the future home that God is preparing for everyone who wants it. A loving, mutually sacrificial marriage is, therefore, one of the most persuasive arguments for the Gospel, one of the most irresistible calls to Jesus, that we can possibly make. So remember, your spouse is not your competition. Never. Win. A. Fight.

Action Steps

1. If you're not married, think through the following scenarios, asking, "How would a marriage that is based on mutual submission look different from one based on competition?"

--Adam has a job offer that he wants to take, but Kaitlyn doesn't want to move.

--Emily feels their growing family needs a larger house in a safer neighborhood, but Sean thinks they already have too much debt as it is without taking on a bigger mortgage.

--No matter how many times Gaby asks Jeremy to go to church, he always says no.

2. If you are married, look again at the list of competitive behaviors in marriage (p. 28). How many do you recognize in yourself? Confess these before God, and prayerfully make a plan to change your behavior.

3. Look again at verses 26-27. Do you understand what God is asking of you as a spouse? What can you do to help your spouse become all that he/she was created to be? Make a list.

Chapter 7

There is a Right Way to Fight

I can't dance. That is an established fact. I am generally opposed to stereotypes, but I am white AND Baptist, and perhaps in this case, the stereotype fits. But a friend told me years ago that every married couple has a dance they do whenever there's conflict. She nags. He yells. She cries. He storms out. She calls her parents. He smashes things in the garage. Rinse and repeat. His point to me was, "If you want things to get better, you have to change the dance. You can't control what your spouse does, but you can change how you respond. It takes two to tango, after all. If one person starts acting in a new way, the other will respond differently too."

It was brilliant advice, I thought. I wish I had heard it earlier. Carrie and certainly didn't dance well early in our marriage. Once, in the middle of a fairly heated disagreement, she walked away. That infuriated me, because I wasn't done discussing this immensely important issue (which I have somehow since forgotten). In anger, I kicked a shoe that was lying on the floor in front of our couch (come to think of it, that may be what we were fighting about). The shoe sailed through the air and struck her on the back of her leg just before she exited the room. It was a perfect shot, but not an intentional one; I couldn't have done that if I'd tried. She spun around with a mixture of anger and confusion on her face and yelled, "You threw a shoe at me???" I bellowed back, "No, I did not throw a shoe at you!" (Classic comeback, right?) She slammed the bedroom door. I flung it back open…and put a doorknob-sized hole in the wall. We didn't own that home, by the way. It was a parsonage, which means it was owned by the church where I was pastor. Fun times.

As time went on, we learned to dance differently. I honestly can't remember who made the first move, but it doesn't really matter. We still disagree about plenty of things. But I don't have any recent stories of epic, ridiculous arguments. I'll take that tradeoff.

Did you know that God grieves when His people don't get along with each other? The night before He was arrested and crucified, Jesus prayed that we, His people, would be one, just like He and the Father are one (John 17:20-23). He said that would be our sign to the world that we really did belong to Him. Every book of the New Testament contains some statement about how important our unity is to God. And in Romans 12:17-21, we get solid instruction on how to handle conflicts in a healthy way. You might call this biblical dance lessons:

Step 1: Stop the conflict before it starts. Verse 17 says, *Repay no one evil for evil, but give thought to do what is honorable in the sight of all.* Mark Twain said, "A bulldog can whip a skunk, but it ain't worth it." Then again, maybe Twain didn't actually say that; he tends to get credit for nearly every witty aphorism. But either way, it's true. Even if you think you're right, even if you think you can "win" (whatever that means), most fights just aren't worth it. That's especially true in marriage. We have a choice in how we respond when our spouse does something we don't like. When we repay evil for evil, it's like throwing a lit match into a barrel of gasoline. But if we can learn to behave in an honorable way, even when we're inwardly angry, it will save us from a world of pain.

For me personally, this comes down to four very practical lessons:

1. Most irritations, insults and disagreements should be ignored. Yes, there are times in a marriage when you must take a stand. Your spouse needs to know that a change is needed. But those moments are rare. I have learned that I don't have to challenge everything. We're both happier.

2. Don't be the one who escalates. In every hurtful argument I can remember, there was a very distinct point where I chose to take things to the next level, emotionally. I raised my voice, or I said something that was calculated to hurt her. Once I did that, there was no going back. It's like toothpaste; once it's out of the tube, there's no putting it back in.

3. Sarcasm never helps. Can you prove me wrong? Have you ever used sarcasm in an argument with someone you love, and found that it improved your relationship? As you grow in spiritual and emotional maturity, you'll find you keep a lot of very funny comments to yourself…and you and everyone around you is happier for it.

4. When there is a serious issue to discuss, wait until you're NOT angry. As I said, there are times when you must take a stand. But there are two different ways to handle it. If you bring up your dispute in the heat of the moment, if your thought process just before opening your mouth is, "That's the last time I'll let her say that to me," or "Oh no, that's not gonna work!" your spouse is probably going to be defensive. They're going to feel attacked, and they will deny whatever you are asking them to change, and list a few problems they have with you for good measure.

Or…you could wait until you are calm, plan out carefully the best way to mention this problem to your spouse, and prayerfully, lovingly talk it over. There's no guarantee that will work, but it's certainly a better starting point.

Step 2: Make it right as quickly as possible. Verse 18 says, *If possible, so far as it depends on you, live at peace with everyone.* I love that verse, because it answers all our objections. The two words "If possible" are an acknowledgement that some people will hate you no matter what you do. But the words "so far as it depends on you" keeps us from immediately defaulting to, "He's just a toxic person. No one could get along with him." Have you done all you can to make things right? Have you tried every possibility?

When it comes to marriage, it's important to take responsibility for making things right even if you think the conflict is mostly your spouse's fault. It's important also to do this before you feel like it. Our natural tendency is to wait for them to make the first move. In that way, we feel like we've "won" some small victory. But it's time to change your dance. Next time there are harsh words and hurt feelings, be the first to apologize.

Here's how seriously Jesus takes this relational principle: *So if you are offering your gift at the altar and there remember that your brother has something against you, leave your gift there before the altar and go. First be reconciled to your brother, and then come and offer your gift* (Matthew

5:23-24). In the Israel of Jesus' upbringing, worship of God consisted of offering sacrifices at the temple. But Jesus was telling His fellow Jews that God didn't want their worship if they had unresolved conflict with someone. Think about it: If you have an unresolved conflict in your marriage, and you're waiting for your spouse to apologize before you make any moves toward reconciliation, you aren't walking with God! Do what it takes to make it right as quickly as possible.

Step 3: Don't make your own justice. Verse 19 says, *Beloved, never avenge yourselves, but leave it to the wrath of God, for it is written, "Vengeance is mine, I will repay, says the Lord."* The concept of God's wrath is not a popular one today, even among many devout Christians. Yet it is a part of His character that is praiseworthy. His wrath is an extension of His love. Instinctively, we understand this: Imagine you had an adult daughter who lived with a man who physically abused and emotionally manipulated her. Would you do whatever it took to get her out of his clutches? Would you be willing to resort to force in order to make that happen? Yes you would, because you love her. God's wrath is His hatred of the things that hurt His children. When we feel wronged, we want revenge. But this verse tells us to leave room for God's wrath. I take that literally; if I choose to exact my own vengeance on someone who has hurt me, God sees and says, "Oh, you've got this? Okay, go ahead." I may enjoy a brief moment of perverse satisfaction at seeing my enemy suffer, but that enjoyment will quickly turn hollow. On the other hand, if I choose the path of forgiving my enemy, one of two things will happen: Either my enemy will repent (that's what verse 20 is about…the shame that leads to repentance when we choose to love an enemy), or God's wrath will bring me justice.

I can't say this more clearly: If you're holding a grudge against your spouse, repent. If you are keeping a list of times he has let you down, repent. If you're currently planning a way to get back at your spouse, or if you regularly vent about her to your friends or family, or if you can't talk about him without rolling your eyes, repent. You are sinning against God, and you're destroying your marriage, while making yourself miserable in the process. Let it go. Before God in prayer, forgive your spouse and ask Him to heal your bitter heart.

I realize right now you may think what I am suggesting is impossible. Let me address three key issues: First, forgiveness doesn't mean you're "over it."

Some of us wait until we're no longer angry or hurt to forgive. But forgiveness simply means, "I refuse to strike back or hold this against you in any way. You are free." You can still be angry and forgive. You can still feel pain and forgive. In fact, choosing to forgive is often the first step in overcoming anger and hurt. Second, as I said in step 1, there will be disagreements and issues in marriage that are serious enough they must be dealt with. Simply forgiving and moving on is not enough. There is a way to do this correctly, and I have a suggestion for it in the action steps at the end of this chapter. Third, if you are being physically abused by your spouse, leave and call the authorities. This is for your good and his. Forgiveness does not mean allowing yourself to continue to be hurt.

Step 4: Respond to hatred with love. Verses 20-21 say, *To the contrary, "if your enemy is hungry, feed him; if he is thirsty, give him something to drink; for by so doing you will heap burning coals on his head." Do not be overcome by evil, but overcome evil with good.* This is a command often repeated in Scripture. In fact, Paul here is quoting Proverbs 25:22. Jesus' commands to "turn the other cheek" and pray for our enemies are even more demanding. Yet most Christians rarely even try to obey these commands. Our excuse is, "That's impossible! No one really lives that way." Oh yes they do. Here's just one example, from the book *Peace Be With You*, by Cornelia Lehn:

In 1938, in a Russian prison, about 250 miserable men were herded together in one small cell. Among them was David Braun. Soon David became aware of a Greek Orthodox priest in their midst. The old man had been thrown into prison because of his faith. His peaceful, radiant face made him stand out in that awful place like a candle in the dark. You couldn't miss him. It was probably because of this that he became the target for the sarcastic and blasphemous remarks of two of the prisoners. They were continually harassing him. They bumped into him. The mistreated him. They mocked everything that was holy to him. But always the priest was gentle and patient.

One day David received a food parcel from his wife. When people are constantly hungry, receiving a food parcel is something that can't be described; it has to be experienced. David opened the parcel. As he looked up, he saw the old priest looking at his bread with longing eyes. David broke off a piece and gave it to him. To his amazement the priest took the bread, broke it, and gave it to his two tormentors. "My friend," said David, "you are hungry. Why did you not eat the bread yourself? "Let me be, brother," he answered. "They need it more than I. Soon I will go home to my Lord. Don't be angry with me." Soon after that he died. But never again in this cell did David hear mockery and blasphemy. The old priest, a true servant of the Lord, had fulfilled his commission.

Not only was he following his commission; he was imitating his Lord. Jesus forgave even the men who spat in His face as He died on the cross. More than that, we were His enemies when He chose to die to save us (Romans 5:10). Who does that? Only Jesus. And only He can make you the kind of person who can overcome evil with good. But when it happens, oh the freedom it brings!

The next time there is conflict in your marriage, what will you do to change the dance? Decide on it today…and see what happens.

Action Steps:

1. If you're married, you have a list of things about your spouse that drive you nuts (you know you do!). Write down your list, then categorize it: Put an "X" by the ones that you will learn to live with, and a "check" by the ones that absolutely have to change. (Hot tip: If you have more than two or three "checks," you need to loosen up. Seriously).

2. Select one of your "checks" and prayerfully strategize how you will talk to your spouse about it. Put yourself in his/her shoes. Recognize that hearing criticism, especially from the one you love, is painful. This is especially true if the two of you haven't handled conflict well in the past. So ask yourself, "Knowing my spouse like I do, how could I express this in a way that they feel loved and not defensive?"

Two tips: 1) Let them know this isn't an ultimatum. You're not saying, "Change or I'm gone." This is an attempt to strengthen things in your marriage.

Which leads to the next tip: 2) Open yourself up by asking, "What would you like me to work on?"

3. If the first attempt doesn't go well, don't give up. Pray and strategize a better way to communicate. Now is probably the time to contact a good counselor to help you two work through your issues.

4. When you've covered the "checks," throw away your list.

5. If you're not married yet, go through these same steps with someone you love (roommate, friend, parent, sibling). Develop the habit of handling conflict in a healthy way before you get married.

Chapter 8

Pray constantly for Her

One night in my dorm at the University of Houston, I overheard one of my roommates talking about conversations he was having with fellow engineering students at Rice on something he called a "Message Board." I thought very little about it at the time. Now I know that he was using an early form of the internet. I had no idea that, within a few years, this technology would change virtually everything about my daily life: The way I communicate, pay my bills, get driving directions, watch TV, read books and articles, book vacations, and shop for everything from groceries to Christmas presents. If you had told me then that I would someday carry a pocket-sized device that would give me access to the world's collective knowledge—everything from a mini-biography of Winston Churchill to a video showing me how to change my car's left-turn bulb--anytime I want it, my mind would have boggled.

Yes, I am aware that the internet has also brought new complications—even dangers—to our world. But when I think about that night in my dorm, how I dismissed my roommate's experiences as something of interest only to nerds, I think about prayer. Scripture tells us that a child of God has constant access to God; in the words of Hebrews 4:16, we can *boldly approach the throne of grace* anytime we need. That should change everything about the way we live in a way far more profound than internet technology: How we tackle crises, make decisions, respond to attacks, prepare for challenges, grow emotionally and spiritually, and change the world around us. Yet I am afraid that many of us, including many otherwise sincere Christians, think prayer (outside of emergencies) is for religious fanatics, not for normal folks. How would you feel about a person today who refused to learn how to use an internet browser, a GPS, or a smartphone because "that's computer nerd stuff"? Far more foolish is the Christian who never learns to pray…especially for the people she loves the most.

Now let's talk about marriage: You may recall from our study of the principle of mutual submission in Ephesians 5 that our job in marriage is to help our spouse become everything God created them to be. We need God's power in order to help them grow and blossom, and His power is accessible through prayer. If we never take the time to learn how to pray for our spouse, we can't really say we love them, can we? Please understand: When I say, "pray for our spouse," I'm not talking about praying that God would change them until they meet our exacting standards. This isn't some sneaky way to cover our selfishness in religious camouflage. However, I have learned that the more I pray for my wife, the more I love her. It stands to reason: God doesn't need for us to tell Him what's wrong with our spouse. He already knows! Prayer doesn't give God information, and it doesn't force Him to change His plans. No, prayer is about changing us, not the Perfect One. Prayer is how we get ourselves onto God's agenda. So how do we learn to pray? Well, I believe one of the best ways to learn any skill is by observing someone who is a master. Fortunately, in the letters of the Apostle Paul, several times he writes out the prayers he is offering to God on behalf of his friends. When we read these prayers, we see what life-changing prayer looks like. Let's look at two of those prayers in this chapter.

First, Ephesians 1:15-23: *[15] For this reason, because I have heard of your faith in the Lord Jesus and your love toward all the saints, [16] I do not cease to give thanks for you, remembering you in my prayers, [17] that the God of our Lord Jesus Christ, the Father of glory, may give you the Spirit of wisdom and of revelation in the knowledge of him, [18] having the eyes of your hearts enlightened, that you may know what is the hope to which he has called you, what are the riches of his glorious inheritance in the saints, [19] and what is the immeasurable greatness of his power toward us who believe, according to the working of his great might [20] that he worked in Christ when he raised him from the dead and seated him at his right hand in the heavenly places, [21] far above all rule and authority and power and dominion, and above every name that is named, not only in this age but also in the one to come. [22] And he put all things under his feet and gave him as head over all things to the church, [23] which is his body, the fullness of him who fills all in all.*

In Ephesians, Paul prays that his friends would:

Know God better (v. 17). Notice Paul doesn't pray for his friends to know facts about God; He wants them to know God personally. You can probably think of a friend or mentor who changed your life in a profound way. Maybe it was a parent who passed down the values that shaped your character, a co-worker who trained you in the skills that made you good at your job, or a friend who showed you how to get through the hardest time of your life, or brought you happiness and laughter in one of your best periods. Now multiply that influence times infinity, and you have an idea how powerful it is when we come to truly know God in a personal way. His values become ours, and our character is transformed. He imparts to us the skills and power we need to accomplish more than we ever dreamed. And His love carries through the darkest times, while filling us with joy, peace and a sense of purpose and victory that the world cannot overcome.

Know the hope He gives, the inheritance He has promised (v. 18). "Hope" and "inheritance" are New Testament words that refer to Heaven. "Hope" means a confident expectation of something wonderful that you know is yours, but you don't possess it yet. That's why that term "inheritance" fits so perfectly. It gives us the image of a young woman who knows that her future is secure, because her wealthy parents left everything in her name. Where that analogy breaks down is that when that young woman's parents die, she will be filled with grief. The inheritance won't take away her sadness. But in our case, Jesus has already died in our place. His death purchased our inheritance. For us, death is victory! Imagine if your spouse was filled with hope in his inheritance. He wouldn't make bad decisions because he knows that earthly things don't last. He wouldn't despair when life didn't go the way he wanted. He would feel free to give himself away joyfully to you and others, knowing that anything we do for others is rewarded hundredfold by Christ. Hope changes everything.

Know His great power for those who believe (v. 19). The same power that raised Christ from the dead is ours. No, we can't use resurrection power to do whatever we want (can you imagine what a disaster that kind of power in our sinful hands would be?). Instead, that power enables us to live out His purpose for our lives. The world says, "You can't, because you're not pretty enough, big enough, rich enough." God says, "Watch what I do with this one." Your spouse, in spite of her flaws, is destined to do heroic, world-changing things. Your prayers could help her grow into the person who fulfills her destiny.

Next, let's look at the prayer found in Colossians: 1:9-14, *⁹ And so, from the day we heard, we have not ceased to pray for you, asking that you may be filled with the knowledge of his will in all spiritual wisdom and understanding, ¹⁰ so as to walk in a manner worthy of the Lord, fully pleasing to him: bearing fruit in every good work and increasing in the knowledge of God; [11] being strengthened with all power, according to his glorious might, for all endurance and patience with joy; [12] giving thanks to the Father, who has qualified you to share in the inheritance of the saints in light. [13] He has delivered us from the domain of darkness and transferred us to the kingdom of his beloved Son, [14] in whom we have redemption, the forgiveness of sins.*

In Colossians, Paul prays his friends would:

Know His will through wisdom and understanding (v. 9). His will isn't a fortune cookie or magic 8ball. It's not so much about where we go to school, what job offer we accept, or how we invest our money. Don't get me wrong; we should absolutely pray about those kinds of decisions, and when God has a definite will in those things, He will let us know. But God's will is mostly about knowing what He is trying to accomplish in our lives. It's getting a compelling vision of who God is trying to make us. You should pray that your spouse would know God's perfect will, so that he will be motivated to chase after that beautiful vision of who he was created to be. Pursuing that vision is where the joy and excitement of life are found; too many of us settle for an earth-bound, self-centered vision, and we end up disappointed.

Live a worthy and fruitful life (v. 10). What does "fruitful" mean? An apple tree is meant to produce apples; an avocado tree is meant to produce avocados…and joy for millennials everywhere. If the tree doesn't bear its designated fruit, no matter how beautiful its plumage, we know the tree isn't healthy. So what "fruit" does God design us to produce? Well, we can answer that question with another question: What does God value? He values people above all else. Jesus didn't die on the cross to bring in a bull market or to influence elections. He died to save people. Therefore, the fruit God wants us to produce is love for our neighbors. It's influencing people toward Him. A fruitful life is one in which others say of you, "I owe her so much." "He's the reason I believe in Jesus." "She inspired me to change my life for good." Pray that your spouse would bear fruit in all of her relationships.

Grow in their knowledge of God (v. 10). This is the only request that Paul's prayer in Ephesians has with this one in Colossians. Notice Paul doesn't say, "…that you would know God," but "increasing in the knowledge of God." That indicates we should constantly be growing in our knowledge of Him. God is the only Being in existence who is infinite; we will never know all there is to know about Him. That's what one reason, by the way, that Heaven will never be boring; we will never get to the bottom of how wonderful He is. But in this life, our personal joy, peace, and significance grow as we get to know Him better. Pray for your spouse's relationship with God to get deeper and richer each day.

Be strengthened for endurance and patience (v. 11). Endurance is the opposite of weakness and despair. It means the ability to keep doing what needs to be done, in spite of criticism or discouraging results. Patience refers to the ability to put up with difficult people and love them in spite of themselves. Interesting, isn't it, that Paul doesn't pray that God would remove the difficult circumstances and irritating people from his friends' lives? Instead, he prays for endurance and patience for them. Perhaps he believes that God allows some of those things into our lives for a purpose. Perhaps he trusts that God knows when to remove them from us. At any rate, your spouse needs endurance and patience. Pray for them.

Give thanks joyfully (vv. 11-12). Pray that others would be thankful? Yes, because gratitude is a key to happiness. Grateful people tend to enjoy the blessings they have, whereas ungrateful people are so obsessed with the things they DON'T have that they make themselves miserable. Come to think of it, it's a good idea to give thanks joyfully FOR your spouse, even while you're praying that she would be a more grateful person. The more you express gratitude to God for her, the more you will enjoy her.

Action steps

1. Pick one of these prayers and pray it for your spouse (or, if you're not married, for someone close to you). Substitute your own language if you want, or pray it as is.

2. Ask God to show you what He is trying to do in your loved ones' lives as you pray for them.

--Does he seem to lack purpose and direction? Pray that he would know God's will for his life.

--Is she under a great deal of stress? Pray she would have endurance and patience.

--Is he a complainer? Pray that he would give thanks joyfully.

--Is she in a time of transition (new job, new school, etc)? Pray that she would have God's power to do great things.

3. Write them a note detailing the things you are praying, like Paul does here. This is so much better than simply saying, "I'm praying for you."

4. Most of all, pray that they would know God better. Long after the present crisis is past, He will still be there.

Chapter 9

You Can't Do This Alone

After we had been married a year, we moved to Ft Worth so I could attend seminary. Considering all the issues we had as a couple at the time, a move like that could have been a death sentence for our marriage. Instead, during those three years of seminary, we turned things around. On paper, that doesn't make sense. After all, we moved away from everything familiar. I worked part-time jobs (when I could get them), while attending school, and Carrie worked full-time to pay the bills. We lived in a series of highly sketchy rental houses. The last rent house had no reliable AC or heat, and an infestation of mice. We were very, very poor. So how did our marriage actually improve? A big part of it was the friends we made during those years. For instance, one night, we went with some friends named Pete and Ashley to the State Fair. Like us, they were in Ft Worth for seminary. We had a great time at the Fair that night. But as we got ready to leave, Ashley started feeling bad; that Fair food wasn't sitting well. She asked Pete to get us home fast. After a few minutes on the road, she didn't like the way he was driving. She thought he was moving too slow. (It's a little unfair to tell this story; Ashley was a very level-headed woman ordinarily, but at this moment she was feeling awful, and wasn't herself.) At one point, after she had criticized Pete rather harshly, he said in a very soft voice, "I'm trying to help you, Ashley." I remember thinking about how different my reaction to Carrie would have been if she had been criticizing my driving in front of others. I would definitely have fought back. Maybe I would've even pulled over on I-20 and said, "You can drive if you think you can do better." But Pete was gentle and patient. I knew then that I needed to spend more time around this guy. I wanted to be that kind of a husband, and maybe some of his patience and humility would rub off on me.

Here's something I encounter again and again as a pastor: A middle-aged man or woman lamenting to me, "I don't understand it. I raised him in the church. He knows how important it is. And his wife grew up in church too. But now that they're married, they only show up at Christmas, Easter, Mother's Day, or when I make them feel guilty. I'm going to start picking up their kids and bringing them to church myself. Their mom and dad may not care whether my grandkids know Jesus, but I sure as heck do." Perhaps you're one of those couples. You feel that sense of guilt about rarely attending church, but it's not enough to motivate you to change. Or maybe you tried for a while, but didn't get much out of it. On the other hand, perhaps you didn't grow up in church, and you think it's bizarre to suggest that a weekly trip to a religious event would make a difference in the state of your marriage. When you put it that way, you have a point. Simply attending a worship service probably won't help. But becoming part of the Body of Christ will make a huge difference. What do I mean?

Proverbs 27:17 says, *As iron sharpens iron, so one person sharpens another.* When I was a kid, my Grandpa—my mother's dad—carried a pocketknife. That wasn't unusual; those were the days when most men carried a knife. But to my brother and me, that particular pocketknife was the sharpest object on earth. We would watch those old commercials in which a Ginsu knife sliced through a Coke can and smile; that was nothing next to what we'd seen Grandpa's knife do. Many a young bull calf had seen his life profoundly altered by that knife; Grandpa had "steered" him in a different direction, if you know what I mean. But Grandpa's knife wasn't sharp because of the way it was made. It grew sharp by constant contact with another hard surface. Grandpa sharpened that knife so often, in fact, that the blade was narrow, about half an inch wide. Other men carried big, impressive-looking blades, but my brother and me both believed that Grandpa's little, worn-down pocketknife was the deadliest piece of metalwork on earth…because it was sharpened so often.

You get the point. We grow through contact with others. And not just the sort of "Hey, dude, how's it going?" contact that is comfortable for most of us. We need to get close enough to another person that the relationship alters us fundamentally. We need for someone to be able to inspire us, to influence us, to encourage us, and even at times to confront us. Makes sense, right? So why do so few of us do this? There are two things about that image of a knife being sharpened that explain why most of us don't seek out help: Effort and change. It takes effort to form these kinds of relationship, and we'll have to be willing to change. Can you trust me on this? It's worth the effort. And you need to change.

You may respond by saying, "Okay, but I have plenty of friends. What does this have to do with the Church?" While any good friend can be a positive influence on your life, there is a type of growth that can only happen through Christian fellowship. Paul in Ephesians 4:14-15 writes, *Then we will no longer be infants, tossed back and forth by the waves, and blown here and there by every wind of teaching and by the cunning and craftiness of people in their deceitful scheming. Instead, speaking the truth in love, we will grow to become in every respect the mature body of him who is the head, that is, Christ.*

Picture a toddler, with a big, round head supported by a wobbly body. Can you imagine if an adult had the same physical proportions? Physical health requires that the child grows into his head. For us as Christians, our Head is Jesus. Quite frankly, we don't match up to Him. We are far less humble, gracious, courageous, and righteous. So how do we change that? Ephesians 4 is an entire chapter about living as part of a faith community; not just "going to church" but investing in one another's lives. That's how we grow into our Head. It happens as we speak the truth in love—which means that timid people must learn the boldness to confront their fellow believers who are straying, and opinionated people need to learn the humility to do it in a way that persuades instead of insults the hearer. Those things happen in community. We learn from each other. The one advantage that a church has over an athletic team, dance troupe, rock band or military unit is the Holy Spirit—and that is a significant advantage. Since the Spirit of God is in us, when we do the hard work of building community with other believers, the natural result is that we all grow. And that growth turns out to be great for our marriage. That's why our friendship with Pete and Ashley—and several other great young couples—was so key to improving our marriage during a challenging period. And it's why you should seek those relationships as well.

Let me take this a little further. You may be aware that people who attempt to climb Mount Everest always hire a guide. These guides are usually members of an ethnic group known as Sherpas, a people group that has existed in the Himalayas for centuries. Why Sherpas? These people tend to have a greater lung capacity—thanks to living their whole lives at high altitudes—so that when you and the rest of your party are oxygen-deprived and confused, they will still be clear-minded. They have also been there before, so they know the safest route up and down the mountain. And they won't just keep climbers alive; they also know the best vantage points along the journey, so that the team won't miss spectacular, once-in-a-lifetime sights. Here's what I'm getting at: It's not enough to have friends; you need friends who are believers, so that the Holy Spirit can bless that friendship to produce growth in you. It's not enough to just attend church; you need to actually know people well enough to "speak the truth in love" to them, and they to you. And it's not enough to simply have "Christian friends." Find some "spiritual Sherpas." Find some Christians of greater spiritual capacity, people who are strong in areas where you are weak, like I did with Pete. Find some who have been there before, people who have been married longer and can teach you lessons they've learned—both about mistakes to avoid and blessings to enjoy along the way.

Along those lines, I wanted to devote the rest of this chapter to something special. My own church is blessed with some incredible married couples. Just knowing them and observing their relationships has blessed my marriage. I spoke to several of our couples who have been married for over 50 years, and asked, "What one piece of advice would you give to married people?" They offered me more than just "one piece" of advice, as you'll see. Take a moment to read through these words of wisdom from people who've developed greater capacity for love, who've been to the top of the mountain and know the way:

Ben and Joyce Sinclair were married in 1956. Ben spent his high school years in Texas and is one of the Junction Boys who played for Bear Bryant at Texas A&M before going on to a career in the oil industry. Joyce is a Texas girl, Baylor graduate, homemaker and mother of three sons of whom she and Ben are very proud. Ben and Joyce exude a Christ-centered humility that is especially amazing, considering how much they've accomplished, and how many lives they've touched. This is combined with a compassionate heart that led them to serve for years in our ministry to the homeless. Whenever I spend time with Ben and Joyce, I walk away inspired.

Joyce wrote: My word of advice to people contemplating marriage is "Don't take it lightly." A prevalent attitude toward marriage among many young people these days sounds like this, "Let's give it a try. If it works out, great, if not, we'll say goodbye and move on". That sounds to me to be a sure recipe for failure. Marriage is intended to be a sacred, life-long relationship between two people (usually involving having children), both of whom promise to be committed to do their best to make it work out and dedicated, with God's help, to giving it the time and attention it deserves.

Ben wrote: Marriage is a lifetime commitment – be as sure as possible of your decision. Seek God's will – be receptive. Putting His will first is the best way to assure and enjoy a full, loving, productive and contributing life, especially as it relates to one's marriage. There will be rough spots – things that require compromise. Involvement in a church and its ministries is important in living out your commitment to God, your marriage and your family.

Don and Janice Archer were married in 1963. Both grew up in Oklahoma. Don was a teacher and coach who is still active in mentoring younger coaches. Janice raised their three kids, then went back to school and finished her degree in education on her 38th birthday. She is one of the leaders of our women's ministry. Don and Janice are the sort of people every pastor wants in his church: Always ready to do the hard work without being asked. They wrote:

1. Remember your wedding vows that were spoken to each other before God and in front of families and friends. The vows of love are a promise to each other and God to last until death.

2. Before marriage you usually see the best side of your mate. It's important you know your mate as much as you can before marriage, because eventually you will see different characteristics, attitudes, thinking, and emotions in your mate. Accept each other as they are. Don't try to change them - they can only change themselves if they want to, but God can change them. Now this can only be accomplished in giving and lifting that mate up through prayer and through God's love and compassion. This takes patience. Love your mate more than you love yourself. Pray for each other and with each other. Make God the center of your home.

3. Communicate with each other - you will have disagreements and arguments - yelling doesn't accomplish anything. Also the tone and the way you say things can have more meaning than what was said. Sometimes it's better not to say anything at all in anger, but it's better to calm down and talk about the situation letting your mate know how you feel. Saying "I'm sorry"

is not a sign of weakness. "Asking forgiveness, what can I do, or what can we do", is a start to communication. Pray over the situation. Respect each other thoughts and feelings in talking things out. Make decisions together.

4. Don't assume your partner can read your mind. If you need help with something, ask for it. Don't pout if your mate doesn't help you do something that you think they should be doing without you asking. Ask them for help when needed.

5. Always be truthful in what you do and say. Don't go behind your mate's back and hide something that you bought. Many live on a tight budget.

6. You don't always have to be right!

7. Humor goes a long ways in a marriage.

8. Find Christian friends that love God and are looking to seek more of Him.

9. Find a church and be a part of that fellowship.

10. Tell your mate you love and appreciate them. Show them affection.

11. Read Galatians 5:22-26, Philippians 2:1-5

Bud and Brenda McGuire were married in 1963. Both are highly intelligent, natural leaders, and strong people. Conventional wisdom says that such a union wouldn't work, but they've done far more than survive; they have built something beautiful. Bud is an outstanding Bible teacher and Brenda is one of our women's ministry leaders. Bud wrote:

First, we believe that the potential for a long and happy (mostly ☺) marriage is established before marriage is contemplated. We grew up in a culture where long marriages were the norm, not the exception. Almost all of our older relatives were still married to their first spouse. Divorce was rare and socially unacceptable. There seemed to be a sense that divorce was a reflection of some moral failure. So, everyone took marriage seriously and expected it to truly be "til death do us part".

A successful marriage must have shared values. Many marriages we have witnessed in the succeeding generations we knew had slim possibilities of success because the partners did not share the same values.

I suppose the best advice we can give is that each partner in the marriage must be more concerned about their spouse than they are of themselves. They must care more for their spouse than they care for themselves. We often in times past, before we learned to read each other better, wound up doing something or being somewhere neither of us wanted to be because we each thought the other one wanted to be there or do that. That seems minor but it illustrates the point.

This, of course, is exactly what Paul had in mind when he wrote Ephesians 5:22-33. He asked for mutual submission…wives submit to your husband; husbands love your wives more than you love yourself.

One other thing, there will be problems in any marriage. Disagreements will occur. Do not throw in the towel. Remember why you are in the marriage and why you took your vows. Work it out! Guys, remember that Christ gave himself for the church and you are to love your wife as Christ loved the Church. Ladies, it is not necessary to always be right. I can tell you a story of how Brenda was submissive and it resulted in making me feel lower than a worm's belly and changed my sorry attitude at the time.

I will finish by saying it has been easy for me, Bud, to be happily married to Brenda. What's not to love about her? It has been significantly harder for her to be happily married to me, Bud. But we really meant it when we said "I do".

David and Becky Greenfield were married in 1970. Both are lifelong public school educators. Becky still serves in our children's ministry, and David is our current chairman of the deacons. The Greenfields are the sort of couple who somehow manage to make you feel like the most important person in the room. David wrote:

NEVER stop pursuing your spouse! Prior to our wedding day, and for a while after we married, I wanted to impress Becky in every way I could. I wanted to take her to fancy or fun places and to do things that I thought she would enjoy doing. I wanted to wear clothes that I thought she would like, and to talk about topics in which she was interested. This way of life continued for several years, and then it began to diminish.

At some point, years down the road of life, I happened to be reading a book about relationships. I then realized that, according to the book, I had developed the attitude that I had psychologically and forever won Becky's love which meant that I no longer needed to impress her like I did in the early years. We also had children at that point which seemed to require much of our love and attention, leaving a little less of that for each other.

Our jobs, and even our responsibilities in church, played a role in distracting us from each other.

So, after the kids were grown and on their own, that empty nest void left us wondering if that was it. We seemed to be looking at each other and asking "What do we do now?" That question lead to reading and searching for answers. And with the searching and much prayer, we were reminded of the excitement and passion of those early years. We began to return to the weekly date nights. We began going to football and basketball games together as well as movies, plays, and concerts. And we could finally afford to eat at nicer restaurants.

Now grandkids have given us a brand-new source of entertainment and joy. Only this time, we remember the need to enjoy them <u>together</u> rather than let them distract us from each other. Now we take them with us to games, movies, and restaurants.

So now, I continue to pursue Becky and she continues to pursue me. We hold hands everywhere we go. I enjoy holding her hand as much as I did on our first date. Her hands are just as soft now as they were back then. I tell her how pretty she is as often as I can, because she is. I help her with housework and she helps me with various projects around the house, mainly because we enjoy being with each other. We enjoy the spontaneity that we did in our younger years. And as we encounter difficult issues in our lives, we find that providing support for each other is just another avenue of pursuit.

My mom and dad had been married 35 years before they divorced. All those years they seemed happy to each of us 6 siblings. Looking back though, I don't think they had continued to pursue each other like they must have before us kids were born. Maybe they were just going through the motions, I don't really know. But the greatest lesson I have learned from their experience is, never take your marriage for granted. Do whatever you can to keep the fires lit.

God made a wife for Adam and gave her to him. I can't help but think that Adam must have been totally awestruck with Eve. God surely made Eve as special and beautiful as any creature He had ever created. To share that feeling with your spouse would go a long way to motivating a never ending pursuit of that person. So I would highly recommend to a newly married couple to remember the special feelings they have for each other at this point in their relationship. Just keep God in the middle, and NEVER stop pursuing your spouse!

Tom and Diane Ribble were married in 1957. Originally from Illinois, they moved here for work. The Ribbles exude an infectious sort of joy. It's clear they love each other and truly enjoy life, and life's more fun for all of us when they're around. Tom wrote:

It takes three to make a marriage work: God, husband and wife. A marriage is a WE thing, it is not a mine or your thing. Keep love alive by staying best friends and enjoying each other's interests but also share some of the same interests. A good balance is a must. Social friendships are important. Choose friends from your church family. Fun memories connecting with couples and raising families together. Also keep in touch with socializing with other friends, co-workers, and neighbors.

Jay and Doris Sims were married in 1971. Jay had a successful career in engineering, and Doris… Doris was on the Search Committee that brought me to our church, and Jay was the Chairman of Deacons my first two years here. The Sims have a passion for passing along the saving love of Christ and investing in the next generation. Doris wrote:

The main piece of advice is to have the Lord first in your life. As individuals and as a couple, you should always be seeking and serving the Lord. Know that marriage does get tough sometimes. A couple should recognize that not only did they make a vow to each other, but they made that vow before the Lord and it is not to be taken lightly. Jay's advice – Give it one more day. Doris's advice – Don't try to change your spouse, instead pray for the Lord to change you and your understanding. Finally, work as a team. This is the advice we gave to our son and daughter-in-law knowing they understood the first two pieces of advice. We feel teamwork is the key to our marriage. We work together in everything – finances, children, church, etc. We do individual things and have individual interests, but we support each other in those things, as well. We are a team.

Action steps:
1. If you are not currently involved in a local church, find one.
2. If you're in a church, but not involved in the small group ministry, take that step.
3. Pray that God would put people in your life who can "sharpen" you. They might come from your church small group.
4. Look for your "Sherpas," the high-capacity people who've been there before you (like the couples we just heard from).
5. Invest in those relationships. Schedule time to be together (both individually and as couples). Learn from them. Let them speak truth into your life without responding defensively. And make the relationship mutually beneficial by doing thoughtful things for them.

Chapter 9 ½

Randomness

There are lots of other things I'd love to say to my younger self, but which didn't merit an entire chapter…or in some cases, would require a whole new book to explore thoroughly. I decided to cheat and throw them all into this (sort of) half-chapter. Do with them what you will.

Leave your parents (and everyone else) out of it. The story of the first marriage in Scripture ends with these words: *Therefore a man shall leave his father and mother and cleave to his wife…*(Genesis 2:24, KJV). Of course, these days most people have long since moved out of mom and dad's house by the time they get married. But the point is still the same. Once you are married, that is your most important human relationship. Don't do anything to make your spouse feel they come in second to your parents or anyone else. Of course, you still need to have healthy relationships with your extended family and other friends. Enjoy the time you spend with them. But your first loyalty is to the one you married. When he makes you angry, don't call your mom or text your best friend. When you do that, you poison his relationship with the other important people in your life. They are likely to resent him long after you've gotten over your hurt feelings. And he'll feel your actions as a personal betrayal, a public airing of your dirty laundry. On the other hand, if your spouse is angry at her parents or other extended family, let her vent. But don't agree with her or pile on. Never put your spouse in the position of having to choose between defending her loved ones or agreeing with you. No one wins.

Get help when you need it. On the other hand, most marriages need help at times. There are fantastically talented, wise and empathetic men and women whose calling in life is to help couples walk through their difficulties. For years, there was a stigma about counseling of any kind. Fortunately, people are beginning to realize their mental and relational health is just as important as their physical health. You wouldn't try to "tough out" a broken arm, and you shouldn't expect deep disagreements in your marriage to magically work themselves out, either. In the same way, take care of your mental and emotional health. Don't hesitate to see someone for depression, anxiety, or other issues, any more than you would ignore a ruptured appendix. Spend the money, take the time, humble yourself, and get some help. And don't wait until you've got your bags packed and the divorce attorney on hold; sit down with a counselor when your issues are fresh.

Be generous. It's counter-intuitive, but if we give 10% of what we make to God (as His people have been doing for centuries) it actually reduces our financial stress. Carrie and I experienced this over and over again. We tithed (that's the biblical term for giving 10%) even when we were barely able to pay our bills. Two things happened: We always had enough to get by, and we never fought over money. Later, as we started to earn more, we were able to go beyond tithing, to be generous in other ways. Sometimes that meant contributing to good causes outside our church. Other times, it meant blessing some family or individual we knew. Why does generosity lead to peace in your marriage? I think there are three reasons: First, it helps us realize our money and possessions actually belong to God. Second, it makes His Kingdom our focus. Jesus, after all, said *Where your treasure is, your heart will be also* (Matthew 6:21). When we give our treasure to God, it changes our heart. Third, He has promised to provide for us if we obey Him in this (Malachi 3:10). Again, I know how much this goes against conventional wisdom. I know many of you have very little financial margin. All I am suggesting is that if you take the time to manage your spending so that you can afford to begin giving to God, you will not regret it.

Keep your finances together. I'm sure there are convincing arguments for maintaining separate bank accounts. But I've never heard one that convinced me. There shouldn't be secrets in your relationship, not even (especially) when it comes to money.

Set some financial boundaries, and stick to them. Carrie and I are far from financial geniuses. But here are a couple of decisions we made early on that have paid off. First, we agreed that we would pay our credit card bill in full every month. Second, we agreed that neither of us would ever spend more than $50 on any purchase without consulting the other first. Of course, $50 today isn't what it was when we got married, so I'm not saying that should be your boundary. And it's very likely that one or both of you entered marriage with some credit card debt, so that requires a different sort of conversation. My point is that you need to be on the same page financially. Take some time to talk things over and set expectations, then stick to them. Sticker-shock is not good for your marital health.

Avoid porn. I cannot overstate this: Pornography is killing marriages. I cannot tell you how many Christian men I've met with in the past ten years who are addicted to porn. In fact, I've had that conversation so many times, when a man asks to speak to me privately, I expect it to be about that. None of this should surprise us. It's so accessible these days, and our culture says it's harmless fun. I disagree. It is inherently disrespectful to the humanity and dignity of women, warping your relationships with every female in your life (I've seen some research that indicates porn use is rising among women, too). It creates sexual expectations that no actual relationship can fulfill. And it is ruthlessly addictive. Avoid it like the plague that it is. If it's already part of your life, deal with it now. There are resources to help you; start by speaking to a minister or counselor.

Team up on your kids. There was a time when I was a parenting expert. I knew more about child-rearing than anyone else I knew. I should have written a book then, because when our first child was born, that know-how vanished. If you think building a strong marriage is hard, wait until you have kids. Parenting is rewarding indeed, but it is also very humbling. Even if your marriage is solid, if you and your spouse aren't on the same page in your parenting philosophies, a good relationship can be strained in a hurry. Communicate with each other. Back each other up; don't fight in front of your kids. Present a united front. Carrie and I have a weekly breakfast together. We go to a restaurant, order coffee and pancakes, and talk face to face. We've spent many of those breakfasts going over "parent strategy." We've made our share of mistakes, but we've stuck together so far.

Pray for your own faithfulness. I adore my wife. She is so much more than I deserve. And I would rather die a violent, agonizing death than be unfaithful to her. When I think of the betrayal she would feel, and how it would devastate my children, and how it would hurt our church, and what it would do to people to whom I've ministered through the years… Yet at the same time, I dare not think I am incapable of adultery. I've known too many good men, many of them ministers, who have stumbled in this way. So I pray often that God's Holy Spirit would guard my heart. The fruit of the Spirit is faithfulness, after all (Galatians 5:25-27). There are other "moral fences" I set up to protect our marriage, but it starts with prayer. I would encourage you to do the same.

Feelings follow action. For some of you, this may be the most important thing you read in the entire book. In the next (and final) chapter, we'll see that the biblical definition of love has nothing to do with how you feel, and everything to do with how you choose to treat someone. But that doesn't mean feelings are irrelevant. It's vital to love your spouse, but it's also important to like her. Sometimes in marriage, we wake up and realize, "I don't like my spouse anymore." If this happens to you, don't despair. This doesn't have to be the end. In fact, it can be the beginning of a miracle. My advice is to love your spouse, even if you don't like her. You can't control how you feel. But you can control what you do. Begin doing things that show her love. See how many thoughtful acts you can perform each day. Pray for her. Compliment her. Make her coffee in the morning; bring her lunch at work. Do the dishes before she asks you. Put the kids to bed when she's too tired to think. You see, there is a hidden genius in Jesus' command to *Love your enemies and pray for those who persecute you* (Matthew 5:44). The Lord knows that we can't go on hating someone who we're praying for and treating with intentional kindness. In fact, the more we love that person, the more we will start to feel affection for them. No, it's not as easy as complaining, or pining for the happy days of yesteryear. But it's much more effective. Love her until you like her again.

Chapter 10

Love Don't Come Easy

And so we arrive at our final chapter, and appropriately enough, it's focused on the "love chapter" of the Bible, 1 Corinthians 13. My money says over half of you who are married had this passage in your wedding ceremony. Probably all of you have attended at least one wedding where this chapter was read aloud. But here's the ironic truth: 1 Corinthians 13 isn't about romantic love. And that's okay, because a lack of romantic love isn't the problem in most marriages. Flowers, candles, spontaneous trips to exotic places and John Legend music may be the stuff of warm fuzzies, but aside from a nice memory or two, they don't make a lasting difference in the quality of your relationship. Because those things (okay, get ready for this) aren't love.

Now, assuming you haven't thrown the book away after reading that last paragraph, you may be asking, "How do you know 1 Corinthians 13 isn't about married love?" One word: context. Take a moment to read 1 Corinthians 12, and you'll see what I mean. Remember, 1 Corinthians is a letter written by Paul to an actual church. In the church at Corinth, there were a number of problems, but one of the most pressing issues was a lack of unity. There were people in the church who, frankly, thought they were better than other church members. For some, it was because of greater wealth and success in life; for others, it was because they had certain spiritual gifts that "lesser" members didn't possess. In chapter 12, Paul wants them to see that the church is like a human body—the Body of Christ. Every part is important. Just as you and I wouldn't want to choose which of our four limbs to be hacked off with a machete, so within each church, we should value every member equally. That leads to chapter 13, in which Paul asserts that if we don't love each other, our financial success and spiritual giftedness is worthless. Love trumps all. Then he proceeds to define love. This is why, in spite of the fact that 1 Corinthians 13 isn't about romantic love, I heartily approve of it being read at weddings. Because again, what we need is not more infatuation; we need more genuine love. And love don't come easy. Take a fresh look at these words:

If I speak in the tongues of men and of angels, but have not love, I am a noisy gong or a clanging cymbal. ² And if I have prophetic powers, and understand all mysteries and all knowledge, and if I have all faith, so as to remove mountains, but have not love, I am nothing. ³ If I give away all I have, and if I deliver up my body to be burned, but have not love, I gain nothing.

We think this is such beautiful, eloquent language, but I doubt the Corinthians thought so. In these words, Paul is describing them, and telling them they are nothing. He's tearing down everything they have built their self-worth upon. If he were writing this to a present-day church, he might say, "If I preach sermons that convert thousands and build a church that draws in an entire city, I'm nothing. If I donate money that sends kids to school and funds research that ends diseases, I am nothing. If I personally sacrifice myself to save others, I am nothing."

How can this be? The great preacher Charles Spurgeon once told a story about a farmer who grew an enormous carrot. He was so impressed by the carrot's size, he carried it to the palace and presented it to the King as a gift in honor of his royal magnificence. The King was wise enough to see that this was a truly sincere gift, so he was generous: "You are such a gifted farmer. You deserve the best land of all. Move your family to the plot of land next to the palace, and farm it for me." The farmer was overjoyed, but a nobleman standing in the court thought to himself, "If that's what you get for a carrot..." The next day, the nobleman came to the palace with a beautiful stallion. He said, "O sire, as you know, I am the Kingdom's greatest horse breeder, and this is my finest stallion. I give it to you today in honor of your glory." The King was wise enough to see the nobleman's greedy heart, so he simply said, "Thank you." The nobleman said, "Sire, I don't understand. You gave that farmer a prime piece of property for his silly carrot, but for my costly gift, I get nothing?" The King said, "The farmer gave me his carrot. You gave yourself that horse." No matter how extravagant we are, if our efforts are self-centered, God is not impressed.

[4] Love is patient and kind; love does not envy or boast; it is not arrogant [5] or rude. It does not insist on its own way; it is not irritable or resentful; [6] it does not rejoice at wrongdoing, but rejoices with the truth. [7] Love bears all things, believes all things, hopes all things, endures all things. [8] Love never ends.

If Paul described the Corinthians in verses 1-3, here he's describing everything they weren't. They weren't patient with one another. They weren't kind. They were arrogant, rude, irritable and resentful. Their "love" was conditional. Again, they were like children. Once, when our kids were very young, I had a brilliant idea. It was Christmas time, and our church was collecting goods for shoeboxes to send to Operation Christmas Child (it's a great program, one that I highly recommend: check out samaritanspurse.org for details). I decided to take both kids to a department store to select items to put in a shoebox. I explained that these boxes would be delivered to kids in poorer nations, who might otherwise not have anything for Christmas, and that by sending them these boxes, we were telling them about the love of Jesus. Unfortunately, the outing turned into a disaster. Both my kids complained about buying toys for other kids, and not getting anything for themselves. Their attitude made me grumpy, and I lost my patience with them. I went into that night thinking I was "Dad of the Year" and ended feeling like a colossal failure as a parent. My kids are both grown now, and wonderful young adults...who will probably kill me in my sleep when they read this paragraph. My point is that small children have a hard time loving others. They can show flashes of sweetness, but for the most part, they think of themselves first. That leads to being easily irritated, and incredibly stubborn. It leads to outbursts of anger and silently holding grudges. The opposite of love isn't hate; it's a childish self-centeredness that evaluates everyone based on "how happy you make me." Love is setting people free, seeking the best for them at great personal cost; the opposite is a neediness that seeks to use people for your own purposes. That has to be overcome, Paul says, or the Corinthian church is doomed.

By the way, when you see the words, *love never ends,* you may be confused. After all, love seems to end all the time in our world. Friendships wither and die. Passionate love affairs flame out. Families fall apart. Loved ones pass away, and we never see them again in this life. So what does Paul mean? The Greek word he uses refers to a city under siege which refuses to surrender. Paul is saying that true love holds on, never gives up, never waves the white flag no matter what. It won't always be easy, but love never surrenders.

As for prophecies, they will pass away; as for tongues, they will cease; as for knowledge, it will pass away. ⁹ For we know in part and we prophesy in part, ¹⁰ but when the perfect comes, the partial will pass away. ¹¹ When I was a child, I spoke like a child, I thought like a child, I reasoned like a child. When I became a man, I gave up childish ways. ¹² For now we see in a mirror dimly, but then face to face. Now I know in part; then I shall know fully, even as I have been fully known. ¹³ So now faith, hope, and love abide, these three; but the greatest of these is love.

The Corinthians loved spectacular things. They assumed that people who possessed impressive spiritual gifts, like the ability to work miracles, utter prophecies, communicate with God in unknown, angelic languages, or who possessed certain "secret" knowledge were more loved by God than "ordinary" Christians. In the same way that a small child is fascinated with a shiny toy but ignores a book that could enrich his life, the Corinthians inflated the importance of "looking spiritual" instead of focusing on the true sign of intimacy with God: The ability to love. In that sense, Paul is calling them two-year-olds. He wants them to admit that they need to grow up and leave their childish ways behind them.

Verse 12 is an amazing promise. Someday, we will fully grow up into the image of Christ. We won't be like children anymore; we'll know as He knows, love as He loves. Love is what it all comes down to. There is a reason why, when Jesus was asked to name the greatest of all the commandments, He didn't answer with any of the things we typically associate with religion. He didn't say, "Go to church faithfully," "Give your money generously to the Lord's work," or "Don't drink, smoke, cuss or chew, or go with girls who do." He said, *Love the Lord your God with all your heart, all your soul, and all your mind…and the second is like it: Love your neighbor as yourself. All the Law and the Prophets hang on these two commandments* (Matthew 22:37, 38-39). Love is the ultimate sign of a transformed heart. Religion certainly has a purpose, but it can be faked. Any of the other commands can be obeyed by someone who, deep in their heart, is hateful and evil. Love is real. Love can change the world. In fact, it is literally the only thing that can.

So what does this have to do with marriage? Consider this section the "Action Steps" of this final chapter:

1. This is a radical redefinition of love. In this definition, love has nothing to do with how you make me feel. It has nothing to do with you making my life better. Instead, it is entirely about me wanting what's best for you. It's about sacrifice. It's about dying to self. It is not a feeling; it's a decision. Don't get me wrong, the feelings of infatuation you feel when you're falling in love are legitimate. They can be a beautiful thing. They can even lead into a more mature affection that lasts your entire life together. But they aren't love in the biblical sense. In fact, if your relationship is entirely based on those feelings, it is destined to fail. You feel the way you do because this person is useful. When they cease being useful—because their looks change or life gets difficult or their feelings for you fade—you won't "feel" any love for them anymore. You'll wonder what happened: "How did our love die?" It died because it was never really love. Love—the kind that never ends—is a conscious choice to do what is in the best interests of the other, even when you don't feel like it. Actually, *especially* when you don't feel like it. To truly love someone is to consistently make that decision, over and over again, for a lifetime.

2. None of us is capable of doing this. No one can love like this, consistently, for a lifetime, no matter how adorable one's partner is. Paul understands that. Note that he doesn't say, "*You* should be patient, kind," etc. Instead, he says, "*Love* is patient, *love* is kind…" This isn't a checklist to make us try harder. Trying harder isn't enough.

3. Now for the good news: There was one who loved in this way. Why did Jesus come into our world in the first place? He certainly didn't have to be incarnated. No one on earth asked God to send us a Savior, to become a human being and execute history's ultimate rescue mission. And even if we had asked, we didn't deserve it. But He came, nonetheless.

Jesus didn't need to call a small group of friends to be with Him daily. He didn't need to invest three solid years of His life in these people. Often, they frustrated Him. Many times, they embarrassed Him. In the end, one betrayed Him, another denied Him, and the rest ran away. Yet He stuck with them in spite of it all.

Most of all, Jesus didn't have to die. At any point, He could have ascended back into Heaven, leaving behind this angry, chaotic pigpen of a world. In His own words, He could have called down legions of angels to defend Him, to wipe out humanity. But He died in our place anyway.

Why did He do these things? It was love. And this is key: He didn't love us because there was anything particularly lovable about us. He didn't love us for how we made Him feel, or what we might do for Him later on. We're talking about someone who washed the feet of the man who had already decided to betray Him, who prayed for the people who spat in His face, who restored the man who denied Him. Jesus showed us a love with no conditions. He loved us because that is who He is.

4. Just like the Corinthians, we are toddlers when it comes to love. We can't grow out of that selfish, childish nature on our own, anymore than a kid can grow taller by wishing for it to happen. We are eternal two-year-olds. There is only one force that can change us into people capable of love. Jesus said in John 3 that our only hope is to be born again to a new life. By the way, He said that to one of Israel's most devoutly religious men, Nicodemus. Essentially, He was saying, "All your religious acts are getting you nowhere. You need to become a new person, and I can do that for you." That event of being born again is what we refer to as salvation. When we talk about it, it's usually in terms of, "I am saved by Jesus, and therefore I will go to Heaven when this life is over." That's true, and wonderful. But it's not all that salvation means.

To truly be a Christian is to be born again. But that is only the beginning. The birth of an infant is a beautiful thing, but that child needs to grow. In my opinion, the problem with American Christianity today is that we've gotten too comfortable in our diapers. We've never really started growing into the image of Christ. Now, if you accuse the average Christian of a lack of growth, they would argue by listing their religious resume: "I go to church faithfully. I read the Bible. I donate to God's work. I volunteer." Yes, but if you haven't become more loving, you haven't actually grown. You've been attempting to buy God's favor for your own purposes through acts of religiosity. You've been using God, not loving Him. Like the nobleman in Spurgeon's story, you've been giving yourself a horse.

5. How do we grow, if it doesn't happen through effort? It starts with repentance. Identify the ways you are childish toward your spouse and other important people in your life. Just think about what makes you angry, irritated or disappointed with them. How does your behavior match up to the standard of love we see in this chapter?

For example:

--A man often hurts his wife's feelings with comments that, in his mind, are only jokes. He can't understand why she hasn't gotten used to his sense of humor yet. But he begins to see that love is kind enough to consider the feelings of others, even when you don't understand them.

--A woman is disappointed in her daughter. The mom was a great student, a star athlete, and popular with virtually everyone on her campus. The daughter, in contrast, is quiet and quirky, dresses like a homeless waif, and spends all her time with a few equally weird friends. The mom says she just wants what is best for her daughter. Slowly, she starts to realize she is disappointed because she was hoping to relive her teenaged years through her. Love is patient enough to love people the way they are.

--In the midst of arguments, a woman finds that she often uses the following sentence: "You always do this!" Of course, it seems true. He always seems to forget important dates. He always seems to leave his dirty dishes on the table. He always seems to have something else to do when it's time to visit her mom. Those are real issues, and they need to be addressed. But she is beginning to see that when she says, "You always do this," it's a self-fulfilling statement. Rather than motivating him to change, it makes him more set in his ways. Love is not resentful; it doesn't keep a record of wrongs done.

--A man finds that he doesn't enjoy fatherhood. On his days off, he makes up excuses to be on the golf course, working in the yard, or anywhere other than at home with his kids. He hopes that perhaps when they are older, they will be more manageable. Then, one day, it occurs to him that he is the problem. After all, love is not irritable.

--A woman can't understand why her husband gets so angry when she tries to help him. She could make his life so much better if he would only listen. Then it dawns on her. He is unhappy because he feels he's married

86

to a second mother, not a wife. He feels controlled, not loved. Love does not insist on its own way.

6. Confess those things to the Lord. Write them down. Be as specific as the examples above. The point is to not make excuses, to not whitewash or rationalize, but to state as bluntly as possible the ways you need to grow in love.

7. Call on the One who loves perfectly to love perfectly through you. This is the power of the Gospel: When we confess our sins and call on His power, we grow into the kinds of people who are capable of loving like He does. It doesn't happen overnight, but it happens. And it is glorious.

Have you ever sung while standing in front of someone who is a world-class singer? Timothy Keller was the Senior Pastor for many years of a church in Manhattan. He had people in his church who sang on Broadway, and others who performed at the Metropolitan Opera. Sometimes in worship, he would find himself sitting in front of one of these uber-talented individuals. He found it was amazing how much better his voice sounded when it had the backing of a powerful, gorgeous voice behind it. In a sermon on 1 Corinthians 13, Keller said this is what it's like when we call on God's power to teach us how to love. After all, when in verse 6 Paul writes that love "rejoices with the truth," the Greek reads this way: *love…sings along with the truth.* Jesus said in John 14:6, *I am the way, the truth and the life.* He is the Truth. He is the only One capable of truly loving. When we sing the song of love on our own, it sounds pitiful. But when we sing along with the Truth, it's amazing how much more beautiful our song becomes. It brings joy to all who hear it, and all who receive it are blessed. As time goes on, the longer we sing along with the Truth, the more we learn to sing it for ourselves. His power and influence transform us. Someday, we'll love perfectly, even as we're perfectly loved. But until that day, we can grow in our ability to sing the song of love to our spouse…and everyone else we know. There is nothing better for your marriage than that.

So who's ready for singing lessons?

Made in the USA
Middletown, DE
17 April 2021